THE

HAPPY REFUGEE

Hummingbird Books

First published on the Internet (and England)

hummingbird-publishing.com

ISBN: 9798411789836

Cover Design - John Stockley
beingjohnstockley.com

THE
HAPPY REFUGEE

Zoltán Mihály

WITH

Steve Eggleston & Mike Powell

Zentrale Anlaufstelle
für Asylbewerber
des Landes
Baden-Württemberg.

~~Verlegt~~

AUSWEIS

To my kids,

Krisztina, Attila, Viktória & Mirella

my wife, Anita

my brother, Tamás

my godsons Kristóf & Zétény

my friends,

and my friends who are not with us anymore

Tamás Szkurszki, Gyula Gulyás, Zsolt Kádár, Péter Kraml.

And my enemies.

CONTENTS

I want to let everybody in my book know in advance that if my stories don't 100% match how they actually happened, it's just because they happened a long time ago and when they did, I was usually drunk, high and stoned and not because I want to overstrain the truth.

INTRODUCTION

O nce upon a time… I really could start my book this way, because so many interesting things have happened to me and my friends that it might seem like a fairy tale. I thought a lot about whether or not to write my story because, as unfortunate as I am about things like this in my life, I suspected it would be more of a headache than a benefit. But as you can see, regardless of that, I just got my head down and started writing.

My children, I dedicate this little book to you because I'm not sure if I'll ever have a chance to tell you in person. I'm thinking mainly of you, Krisztina and Attila, because your 'good' mother didn't allow me to keep in touch with you. Shit happens!

Question: 'What do kids know about their parents?' Think about it! Not much. Especially not about their youth. They know them only as parents. They might tell you some instructive stories of tougher times, but that's not the whole truth. They don't tell of lots of things they've done, because they don't want you to do them; they're afraid you'll get hurt. They think that while it was permissible for them, it will surely go wrong for you. Because they were so different at your age, weren't they?

Of course not. So I thought I'd have some beer and write some stories about my youth. Oh shoot, I'm already lying. I don't know what's wrong with me. I hardly even drink beer, I mostly drink cider. I promise that was the last lie, because the whole point of this story is to tell the truth, even if it's embarrassing – and there have been many embarrassments in my life. But everything that has happened to me in the past determines where and who I am today. So if I think about it, I don't regret most of my actions.

Dear Krisztina and Attila! I'm sorry I can't be your 'dad'. When I was young, I thought I would never have a child because I didn't want to force anyone I love into this shitty world. Unfortunately, selfishness later took hold of me and I could only think of what I wanted and how much I could love a child. As it turns out by now, I can love not just one but four children. Unfortunately, I already know that I haven't been able to help two of you for over 20 years now. I just hope that dear Krisztina and Attila, you are fine! I have failed once as a dad; I hope my second attempt will be more successful. When we parents want a child, we talk to each other, but you kids don't get a say in whether or not you want us as parents.

Parents should make every sacrifice so that their children grow up happily. Isn't that what we want for you kids? The only problem is that this beautiful thought fades over time. We don't try to shape our lives to make yours easier, we try to shape your lives to make ours easier. That's not fair, because you didn't ask to come into this world. We parents wanted you to be here, so we should make every sacrifice to make you feel good and happy in your life.

Read this story with empathy and generosity of spirit. It is true that we parents sometimes forget that we were young, but at least you should not forget that. True, this story is about your dad, but when most of these things happened to me, I wasn't a dad. I was as old as some of you are now – free and irresponsible.

I hope all of you will take or have already taken advantage of your youthful years. Taking life too seriously is uncalled for! After 54 years of experience, my advice is to only devote time and energy to those things that make you happy and feel good. Life is too short to be sad about it, so just be happy. Unfortunately, I forgot about this for several years and I think that is the main reason for losing you, Krisztina and Attila.

What I failed to anticipate were the many factors that weren't up to me/us. Because of that, I apologise! I was – and still am – inexperienced. But I can say with confidence, that you can come to me with any of your problems, no matter what they are. I will do my best to help you, no matter what I have to do. But I want one thing in return. You, as brothers and sisters, must love and help one another.

Maybe asking you to love each other is foolish. I know it doesn't work that way. What I meant was, for each of you to give the others the chance to know and love you. I never thought I would have all this love in me that I could feel for you, but I do.

Just one more piece of advice. As you will see as you read my book, I haven't been the most honest person in the word, but I never lied to people I loved and cared about so I advise you to do the same. You can lie to police and other authorities but never to loved ones and this way you will only have true friends and partners. Of course, you will lose people on your journey of life but they are probably not meant to be with you. Sometimes it will be painful but if you lie you will just lose them later. So why lie?

Anyway, kids, I'm the happiest dad in the whole wide world. I love you so much, my dear Krisztina, Attila, Viktória (Viki) and Mirella (Mimi).

CHAPTER ONE

I WANNA BE SEDATED

When I was a child, growing up in Soviet-occupied Hungary during the early 1970s, I had a recurring dream that I could fly.

I would stand barefoot and nervous on the balcony outside my bedroom window on the ground floor of the four-storey block of flats we called otthon (home).

Then suddenly, I took a leap of faith, kicked off with my skinny legs as if I were swimming breaststroke, flapped my arms wildly and started to levitate until I was high enough to survey the moonlit rooftops of my home city of Szeged near the southern border with the old Yugoslavia.

It wasn't very elegant, but it worked. I was flying! If you've ever had an aerial dream, you'll know the sheer exhilaration and feeling of power that surges through your body.

I could go anywhere I wanted. But for some reason, with a monumental failure of childhood imagination, I'd use my superpowers to glide above the city's historic municipal buildings.

I would fly over the town hall with its ornate patinated roof that looked so minty green, I wanted to lick it. Then I'd sail over the 'Old Lady of Szeged' water tower at the Saint István Square, along the wide avenues of the inner city, past the Móra Ferenc Museum and the National Theatre next door. I'd fly over the oldest building in

Szeged – The Dömötör Tower – in front of the brooding cathedral, with its twin spires, in the huge town square – Dóm Square – the exact same area as the Saint Mark Square in Venice (12,000 m^2), bordered on three sides by The National Pantheon – over a hundred stern-faced busts representing famous grown-ups from Hungarian history, sciences and arts.

Sometimes I'd visit the romantic Bridge of Sighs by Széchenyi Square, built to mimic the famous bridge in Venice, Italy, before buzzing the old Szeged Synagogue, a beautiful 48.5m-high fairy castle built out of gingerbread and white sugar icing, topped off with a huge stained-glass blue-grey dome.

I usually headed downtown to the corner of Tisza Lajos Boulevard and Kölcsey Street where The Reök Palace sat frozen in the moonlight like a giant green-and-lilac art nouveau Christmas cake. I never got lost, because I could navigate using the river Tisza, which flows through the city and turns a corner there (the old Hungarian word for 'corner' is szeg).

Other people say the city takes its name from the Hungarian word sziget which means 'island' or that szeg means 'dark blond' and refers to the colour of the water where the rivers Tisza and Maros meet in the east end of the city.

Often, I'd start feeling cold and would fly back to my warm bed long before dawn, but on a few rare occasions, I managed to explore far beyond Szeged, northwest to our capital, Budapest.

I didn't stop there. I crossed the Hungarian border, flew on to Vienna in Austria, then due west to Stuttgart in Germany, before heading south to Venice in Italy. I just had to blink and I could cover hundreds of kilometres in seconds.

It was awesome, but illegal of course, without the necessary paperwork. Fortunately, the vigilance of the ever paranoid Hungarian authorities could not intrude into my dreams.

Even as a small child, my yearning to travel and seek adventure, seemed to trump my fear of punishment, at least, while I was asleep.

Whenever my flying dreams took me beyond my home country of Hungary, they always ended the same way. First, I would spot my father way down below, dressed in his blue overalls, standing in the street.

My parents, young & happy

He seemed to smile at first, but then his face always turned angry and he'd start shouting at me and waving his arms, which were covered in dirt and motor oil and but I would be too far away to hear what he was saying.

Then I'd start plummeting to earth, my powers of flight now spent, the magic destroyed. I would frantically search the fast approaching ground for a soft landing, like a haystack or even a pond. I never found one and always woke up in a cold sweat just before the impact.

I don't know if those dreams were a premonition of my late teens and early twenties, when I would visit all those cities, as I travelled around Europe as a political refugee with several fake identities and a ten-year prison sentence waiting for me, should I be sent home. They certainly demonstrated that I had a developing thirst for adventure that would eventually land me in deep trouble.

As I look back on that period of my life now, in my fifties, married with my own children and happily settled in Brighton, England, I can't really see how I could have turned out any differently. I have always been a bit of an outsider, although my early childhood was happy enough.

This is me when I was about 4-5 months old (I guess), and extremely cute

I was born on 14th June 1967 in Szeged, Hungary. My childhood was so uneventful that I'm tempted to skip over it, because nothing really happened, I didn't really excel at anything and I couldn't wait to leave school. I think I was always waiting to begin my life.

CHAPTER TWO

I JUST WANT TO HAVE SOMETHING TO DO

Szeged is a magnificent city with lots of impressive civic buildings and culture, including a world class university, but I grew up in a small ordinary flat in a complex of purpose-built flats. I was surrounded by drab concrete.

The city used to have lots of small houses, but the government tore many of them down and built large low-rise blocks of flats in their place. You can see them in Russian movies and they are similar to the council estates that sprang up in London in the late sixties and early seventies.

Our building had three entrances, each entrance served four floors and each floor had three flats, except the ground floor, so they could really pile people in. In our flat, we had one bathroom, a separate toilet, a kitchen, living room, small room ('half room') and a bedroom.

Every evening, my parents pulled out a sofa bed in the living room and slept there. In front of each building of 42 flats, there would be just six parking spaces – two in front of each entrance – but most of those lay empty because hardly anyone had a car.

We existed under what was sneeringly called 'Goulash Communism', with better living standards and more freedom that the rest of the Soviet bloc with the state allowing limited imports of some Western consumer and cultural goods.

I suppose I was very fortunate to have been born during the Post-Stalinist era. By the time I hit my late teens and early twenties, thanks to Mikhail Gorbachev, Hungary was making a relatively smooth transition to a Western-style democracy.

We weren't dirt poor, but we weren't rich either. Most people lived like that. These blocks were cheap to build and packed many people into a small area. So we were an average family living under far less authoritarian control than other Communist regimes but were still under Soviet occupation, which didn't officially end until June 1991. We had general elections, but both parties were 'socialist' (i.e. in this context, Communist), so there was no real choice, rather like in the UK today (only its mirror image), with a hard-right government and a Labour Party under Keir Starmer that looks increasingly like Tory-lite, especially with his recent spate of Stalinist purges of the left-wing of the party.

The very poor people lived in rural areas and scraped a living off the land growing beetroot and calluses and the very rich people were well connected to the government. Everyone lived in the same kind of housing regardless, unless they were very high up in the party. The richer people owned bungalows or few storey houses, and we middle class lived in the purpose-built flats.

If someone was richer, they still lived in the same area. The father of one of my friends was a chauffeur for a high level politician, so he got very good money, but he still lived in the same houses as us.

Only rich people owned cars. We couldn't afford to buy one, but my father was a mechanic and a driving instructor, so he got to run in lots of new models, which was great for us. It meant we could travel around Hungary and go on day trips. My father knew people who had cars, so they brought them to him, because it was cheaper than going to the dealership.

Unfortunately, as I got older, his habitual heavy drinking tipped over into alcoholism and he eventually lost his driving license.

Even if you were rich, there were no fancy cars anywhere in Hungary. The best car you could buy – and only then if you were well-connected and were prepared to wait for years – was the poster child of crap cars for the West. Can you guess what this object of desire was? It was, of course, the Lada. The Soviet dream machine! Ladas were designed to be easily maintained by their owners, but my father still found himself servicing a fair few during his career, despite their reputation for reliability (which in the seventies meant the car only broke down every other journey).

After the Lada, the next best ride was probably the Polski Fiat 125, which was about the same size as the Lada and just as uncomfortable. In Hungary, we nicknamed it 'Nagypolszki' or 'Nagypolák' ('Big Polski'), while the 126 was called 'Kispolszki' or 'Kispolák' ('Small Polski').

Then, in no particular order of shittiness: the Romanian-built hell-on-wheels Dacia; Czech-built sardine tin Škoda and two deathtraps from East Germany: the Trabant (synonymous with the Secret Police) and the Wartburg 353.

On Wikipedia, there's an amusing photo of Romanian communist dictator, Nicolae Ceauşescu slowly driving the first Dacia 1100 in 1968, looking for all the world like he had just soiled himself.

Some enterprising Hungarians would buy one of these cars with the sole purpose of flipping it immediately for half as much again, such was their scarcity. Szeged had a population of about 200,000 and it was the third largest city in the country, but there were no car dealerships. If you could afford a car, you filled in a lots of paperwork with the council and if you were really lucky, you got to choose the colour.

The other thing you had to wait years for was a telephone. My father was lucky enough to get one after being hired as a mechanic to work on government postal vehicles, so this connection meant he got special treatment. His application was fast tracked and hey presto, we got a phone – eleven years after applying! We couldn't use it of course, because we were the only people we knew who had a phone. Only half kidding.

We had a black-and-white television though and a record player with two speakers. The image of Hungary in the West is that it's a harsh dreary place – which is spot on. It really was like that. Thankfully, we were better off than Bulgaria, Romania and East Germany. We were closer to Poland in terms of living standards; we had meat in the shops and almost everything – it was expensive, but it was available. We had meat at the weekend, not so much during the week.

We didn't have any TV dinners; our meals were all home cooked by my mother. Breakfast was usually some toast with just butter or jam or some kind of meat like ham or salami. The Pick salami factory is one of the city's biggest employers, after the university, so we always had locally produced cured meat in the house. There was a rumour going on in Szeged when I was a kid that the original Pick salami was made from donkey meat, but I never found any proof of that. I think by the seventies it was chiefly made out of pigs.

On Sundays we had meat soup, but different from the UK, where the soup is all blended together, like a sauce. We do it differently. All the ingredients are kept separate: chicken/pork/beef, potato, carrot, parsnip, celeriac, garlic, onion. And we also had wiener schnitzel or gulyás or székelygulyás, which is a kind of goulash. It's close to what you might call a farmhouse stew. Szeged is famous for this and also for halászlé, a delicious fish soup made of carp and catfish.

To kill brain cells, we had vodka and beer and a Hungarian speciality called pálinka, but not the good stuff, it was just alcohol and some kind of artificial flavouring. In the villages, people could grow their own fruit and mash it up to make delicious authentic pálinka, steamed in a copper cauldron or érlelt (aged) pálinka, aged in wooden caskets, but if you grew up in the city like me, you had to drink the shitty artificial version; it would get you hammered but it gave you a terrible hangover.

In a country famous for its use of paprika – a spice made from dried, powdered capsicum fruits which is found in almost all Hungarian food – Szeged is known as Paprika Central.

When paprika first arrived in Hungary in the second half of the 16th century it was as an ornamental plant, but it wasn't long before some bright spark stumbled upon its culinary secrets. He or she must have unintentionally spilled some of it into their stew, after having accidentally dried the fruit carefully first prior to inadvertently grinding it into a fine red powder!

The future was looking bright to me

My mother worked because everyone had to have a job, by law. For most of the time I remember she was a secretary or administrator in the personnel department working for a senior citizens home.

We went to school at the end of the street, just a few minutes' walk from the flat. School started early, and there was an after-school homework club if your parents were late collecting you.

From eight o'clock to five o'clock we were in school. After that, and at the weekends, we would be playing outside. There were only two channels on telly, and really shitty programmes so we were outside all the time.

We used to play a lots of football, handball and basketball but I wasn't very good at those. Although, I did love and excelled at kayaking and canoeing and my father did that as a sport when he was young and he was also a coach.

As well as being the home of paprika, Szeged is also known as the 'City of Sunshine' because of its sizzling weather. Summers today are even hotter than when I was growing up. They are an unbearable 34–36 degrees now, which is too much. When I was a kid it was more like 30–32, which is just right.

During the long hot summers we'd always be playing on the river. Our favourite 'beach' on Tisza was called 'Sárga' (Yellow) because of the colour of the water. My parents took us there when my brother and I were young and then when we got older we went there with friends. It was right next to the kayaking and canoeing club and that is why it became our favourite. I'd go swimming in my Speedos – which I recently learned are affectionately known as budgie smugglers. The girls wore bikinis. Everyone was doing lots of sports, because there was nothing else to do, so there was almost no obesity; it was very rare to see.

Our other favourite place was Mártély about 35km from Szeged. There was a lake and a campsite beside it. At a young age, we could ride our bicycles there just for a day trip in about an hour or so. When we passed age 14 we took a driving test for mopeds under 50cc and our parents bought us mopeds. From then on, we drove to Mártély on our little mopeds and stayed in the camp for days.

There were usually four of us, including Lacika, my best friend since kindergarten. After kindergarten we went to the same school and we were in the same class there too until age 14. Lacika was such a good friend that I only went to Vedres István Vocational High School of Building and Construction because he went there. I had no plans for the future so why shouldn't I stay with my best friend? Unfortunately, there we were put in different classes. And there was Ofi and Menyus, who were my best friends from the neighbourhood. Ofi lived two buildings from mine and Menyus in the next building to Ofi's so I have known them as long as I can remember. We grew up together.

Ofi, Menyus & Lacika before celebrating something

These two were a year younger than me but we still went to the same school just like everybody else in the neighbourhood.

We didn't just go camping together, we did everything together. I remember one time, after setting up the tent, we went to the local boozer for a drink. We were 15 or 16 years old and the drinking age in Hungary was 18 but most of the boozer owners or workers didn't care. Maybe that's why we turned out the way we are today.

Anyway, we were having our first beer when Menyus said: 'I know a guy who got drunk from two beers. How cool is that? He doesn't have to spend much money to get drunk'. And what happened next? After our second beer, we had to go back to the campsite because Menyus got so drunk that the boozer stopped serving us alcohol. Ofi and I had to help him to get back to the tent.

While he was resting, we went to the local shop to buy more alcohol. The camp was full of young kids like us and of course there were lots of girls too. Our plan for the night was to pick up girls. So we started drinking heavily to get the courage to speak to them.

Meanwhile, Ofi and I got bored and started to play a game. It was the season for a kind of beetle to come up from underground and fly away. I know what you are thinking: the game was who could catch the most beetles but you are wrong. The game was who could eat the most beetles.

I'm not sure who won the game but we got drunk enough to pick up girls. We spotted two girls and we invited them to our tent. We all sat down outside and started to chat. Everything was fine until we started to brag about how many beetles we had just eaten and who won the game. The girls were polite because they stayed for another 10 minutes but then they found an excuse to leave. Who can blame them? Who wants to kiss a guy who just ate a dozen beetles? By then Menyus had woken up so we decided to go back to the local boozer.

We hopped on our mopeds and rode away. It was a short ride because we were stopped at the gate by the 'gatekeeper'. She didn't let us through because she said: 'You guys are too drunk to walk let alone drive'. We went back to the tent and formed an 'escape plan'.

We always had tools for the mopeds and of course, we had combination pliers too. So we cut the fence and pushed the mopeds through. There was a field between the camp and the town but with the mopeds we could be there in 5 minutes. We pushed the mopeds for a while just to get a bit further from the camp and then we started them up but we kept the headlights switched off so no one would see us. The problem was that we couldn't see anything either. It was very dark by then. Lacika was the bravest, so he was leading us. He had a very small moped, not even a metre high. We were riding behind him when suddenly we saw his moped stop dead as he flew forward. He had hit a small fence that was invisible in the dark. We cut through that fence too and continued our journey with the lights on. Fortunately, we soon reached a ditch and pushed our mopeds through it. It was so deep that Lacika's moped was totally submerged with only his rearview mirror sticking out but we got through that too.

We were almost at the edge of town and the boozer was only minutes away, when my moped stopped. It didn't matter how many times I tried to start it, the engine was dead. I got so angry that I grabbed a piece wood and started hitting my moped and yelling: 'You piece of crap, I'll sell you to the first gypsy I run into for a 6-forint ice cream'.

After this incident, we all pushed our mopeds to the boozer and of course back to the camp too but we had some beers in the boozer so it was all worthwhile. The next morning, when I had sobered up, I noticed that I hadn't turned the fuel lever on so the engine couldn't get fuel and that was why my moped had stopped working. There was nothing wrong with my moped except the damage I caused hitting the fuel tank with a piece wood. I had to fill up my moped twice to get home because the fuel tank was so beaten up it could barely carry any fuel.

OK, let's get back to Szeged. I grew up around the river. As a coach, my father had access to a motor boat to follow the kids as they kayaked and canoed, so we could ride that as well and I felt very privileged – that was a very good feeling. Many kids never got to sit on a motor boat like me.

I also did some wrestling, athletics and karate, but the boating was a big favourite and made me very happy. Karate was also lots of fun. Back then everybody wanted to be Bruce Lee. So, I too signed up at the local dojo, hoping that I could be the next big martial artist, though I didn't even like to fight.

At first everything was going as planned. Lots of running and stretching. Next we were shown some kicking styles to practice. On the third day I thought I knew everything. When the Master asked for a volunteer to fight with a more skilled opponent, I put my hand up, even though I was scared and inexperienced. No matter. I stood up against a powerful opponent to demonstrate my training. I knew he was strong. But so was I. In his second move, the little shit spun around and whacked me in the mouth with a roundhouse kick, breaking my front tooth in half. I decided I'd had enough of karate, so I gave it up after the first week.

I was still a 'good' guy then, I hadn't left school yet. I had signed up for karate with Lacika and we quit together too, but for months we didn't tell our parents so we could keep receiving the money but we spend it on something else.

As it happened, my opponent was Doxen, but I didn't know him very well at the time. We went to the same boozers and discos but with different groups of friends. Breaking my tooth in half was an accident but Doxen felt very bad about it and he wanted to make it up to me but didn't know how. Luckily, for me, he had his chance soon enough.

One night we found ourselves in the same house party. Doxen showed up with a girl named Eszter. He wanted to get off with her but nothing had happened yet. Doxen had noticed that I liked her too because I was always hanging out where Eszter was. Since Doxen was still feeling guilty about my half-broken tooth, he gallantly offered to step aside at the party so I could hit on Eszter. If I managed to get off with her, he would give us his blessing; if not, he would try his luck with her the next day. I liked the idea, so we went to the kitchen where we had left Eszter. In the kitchen were another four guys and we started competing over who was 'brave' enough to down a glass of neat vodka in one.

Even before the 'competition', I sensed that Eszter might have feelings for me, so I knew my time had come. I gazed deeply into her pretty brown eyes as I chugged down the glass of vodka. For seconds, there was dead silence in the kitchen and all eyes were on me, as everyone waited to see what would happen next. Since I couldn't drink any mixer, I had just taken big gulps. I also barfed up some vodka into my mouth, but with great fortitude I swallowed it back down again.

I must have looked terrible because Eszter said: 'Drink something you idiot, before you start to puke all over the place'. I immediately jumped on the tap and drank about a litre of water before I puked all the vodka out. Then Doxen shooed the others out of the kitchen so Eszter and I could be alone.

So, this was how my first sexual relationship began. I'd had sex before and relationships, but never the two together. It was a serious milestone in my life, but even so, it only lasted for about three months because Eszter wanted to be with me all the time which meant I missed out having lots of fun with my friends, especially with Lacika, who was my best friend at the time.

The irony was that I left Eszter so I could spend more time with Lacika and a few weeks later they got together so I was without Lacika again. They were nice about it because they asked me first if I was OK with their relationship but how could I say no – I liked both of them.

Anyway, let's get back to my childhood. There were lots of families and kids so we'd all play together and the parents would all look out for each other's kids. From age six or seven we weren't supervised, we could bike around. We didn't even have to go home to eat, we could stop off at the house of a friend who lived closer.

There was that sense of community, where everyone was watching out for everyone else. I suppose that was true of many countries in the seventies. But if we could eat at a richer friend's house, that was the best result!

Like I mentioned earlier the river Tisza is running through Szeged. Today, if you drive through the inner city, you'll notice that it has really wide avenues. That's because there was a terrible flood in 1879 which killed 165 people and destroyed about 95 percent of the town (only 265 of the 5,723 houses remained standing).

Emperor Franz Joseph visited the town and promised that 'Szeged will be more beautiful than it used to be'. He made sure that a new modern city was built in its place with wide boulevards and in the early twentieth century many beautiful art deco buildings added to its splendour.

Hence, flood defences are an important part of Szeged's infrastructure, not least those that were built to protect the flats where I lived, which ran right alongside the blocks and provided another play area for me and my friends. When the snow came in winter, we could slide down them.

You know kids, because I mentioned earlier, that the TV programmes were shitty, there was no PlayStation, no computers. You could read a book, but I was not a big reader. But we did have cinemas. The first film I remember seeing by myself and which I loved was The Postman Always Rings Twice, which was a blockbuster in Hungary.

Before that, I remember that Star Wars was popular with everyone. I only saw it once as a child, but all the kids used to compete over how many times they had seen that film.

Bored, bored, bored but at least I always followed the latest fashion

Ask anyone who grew up in the seventies and eighties,

whether they lived in Hungary or in the United Kingdom, and they will tell you that they remember long hot summers when they were bored, bored, bored.

Today there are a limitless distractions, from hundreds of television channels, computer games and the bottomless depths of the internet, social media, TikTok, YouTube. There are myriad ways to waste hours on the proverbial boring Sunday afternoon. But back in the seventies I distinctly remember that hollow-restless feeling that would descend on me from time to time, often triggered by a sensory signal, such as the sound of 'Jó ebédhez szól a nóta' ('Folk Songs for a Good Lunch') on the radio as the whole family was eating together every Saturday and Sunday exactly at noon in the kitchen, or the smell of a meal cooking that I didn't really like. Then I would yearn to be somewhere else, anywhere but Szeged.

I wanted to do something exciting with my life, but I didn't know how to make that happen, but neither did I have any great ambitions to do anything specific, towards which I could have focused my energies. For example, if I'd had a childhood dream of being a vet or a doctor, I could have worked hard at school and made my dream come true (I might even have applied myself more, academically). But I didn't have a specific life goal. Ambition without direction is painful; it's a dreadful intangible gut-sickening feeling that all the fun is happening somewhere else in the world of grown-ups, hundreds of miles away. Anyway, that was how I felt, sometimes. Time travels so slowly when you're a child, punctuated by a few things to look forward to, such as birthdays, Christmas and Farsang.

'What's Farsang?' I hear you ask. In Hungary, we don't celebrate Halloween but we do have a festival which involves fancy dress. It takes place post-Christmas through to February, and it's called Farsang (which literally means carnival). In times gone by it would go on for nearly two months with lots of feasting and drinking, mainly because the farmers had little else to do when the ground was frozen solid. It really was a period of no rules, when many winter babies were conceived. It was also like a purging, without the murder!

At school, things were a little tamer, with a fancy-dress competition. Every class had to dress up as something. Kids came up with suggestions for a theme and presented them to the teacher. The best idea was chosen and everyone had to dress up to that theme. One year we did The Wizard of Oz and I was the Tin Man. We won the school competition and received a cake for our efforts.

Another part of the festivities are szalagos farsangi fánk (ribboned carnival doughnuts). They are shallow fried in oil and then flipped, creating a lighter ribbon around the middle – hence the name. Then they are filled with cream or apricot jam and dusted with icing sugar. Delicious.

At the end of Farsang, we would also observe 'Torkos csütörtök' (Fat Thursday), which was a day for eating excess amounts of food, traditionally on the last Thursday before Lent, but now it's after Ash Wednesday. On this day, lots of Hungarian restaurants offer half-price meals to encourage everyone to pig out.

About 160km west of Szeged, is a town called Mohács, where their annual Farsang celebrations have been registered by UNESCO as an 'intangible cultural heritage'. As well as the usual excessive feasting and drinking, music and parades, they have a unique series of events called busójárás, which are intended to scare away the demons of winter.

The busó – men disguised in large woollen coats and carved wooden face masks – sneak up on the townsfolk in rowboats on the river. Then they run riot, playfully chasing people around and causing merry havoc. This is supposed to hark back to when their ancestors thwarted a

Turkish invasion by dressing up as demons and scaring the aggressors away.

Finally, on Shrove Tuesday, a Farsang coffin is burned to symbolise the death of winter to make way for the spring. Then everyone breathes a huge sigh of relief, takes their biggest shit of the year and adds their name to the waiting list for a liver transplant.

CHAPTER THREE

ROCK 'N' ROLL HIGH SCHOOL

At school, we were graded from 1 to 5. If you got 1, meant you failed, 2 you hardly passed, 3 was average, but it meant that you couldn't go on to higher education but had to learn a profession. Getting 4 was great and 5 was excellent. We had a booklet with all the subjects in it and when we were graded, the teacher put the grade in that booklet so our parents could see how we were doing at school. Also, if the teacher wanted to write a message to our parents, that went into that booklet as well. If we were very bad, the head teacher would write a warning in that booklet and after the third warning we were kicked out of school and had to enrol at another, so we lost all our friends. If you did something very good, that went into the booklet as well but in my I only had warnings.

Naturally, the parents had to sign the booklet so the teachers could see that they had read the messages and had seen our grades. We didn't just sit written tests; we had verbal exams too. At the start of every lesson, the teacher called students one-by-one to the front of the class, whereupon they had to tell everyone what we had learned in the previous lesson. The teacher graded this too and so that went into the booklet as well.

The student was supposedly chosen at random for this verbal exam, so you can imagine how big the pressure was on those who hadn't studied. The teacher enjoyed that. For every year group, the teachers had a book which contained the names of every student on a separate page, listing all the subjects and grades. The teachers chose the student for the verbal exam from this book. But they chose very slowly – turning the pages back and forth, taking their time while we students were shitting in our pants. It was very painful. I was/am dyslexic but when I was growing up there was no such thing, just a stupid kid who couldn't read. The teachers really enjoyed calling me out almost every day to read out loud for the amusement of the whole class. That's why I still hate reading. Since then, I don't think I have read more than four books during my entire life.

When you left school at age 14, you could only go to trade school if you had a score of 3 or less, but you couldn't go any higher after that. You couldn't go to university at that level, you became a worker.

When you were 14, you had to choose what you wanted to be, which is hard because it's so young. I wanted to be a building engineer because my friend Lacika went to that school, but it was very labour intensive and took up all my time.

That school was the Vedres István Vocational High School of Building and Construction not just to learn how to lay bricks but architecture as well, and after that I would be able to do another three or four years of further education.

Four years meant university; completing three years meant I was still a building engineer, but at a lower level, where I could design houses but not a movie complex or a high rise. I could design houses and other small buildings, but if I aspired to design hospitals and other big projects, I would have to study in university for four years.

However, there was a small problem: all I wanted to

do during my teen years was to go out and have parties and meet up with friends, but with building engineering I seemed to spend all my time drawing blueprints and learning draftsmanship, both in and out of school. It was relentless.

Also around this time, my father's drinking deteriorated. When I was young it wasn't too bad. He was always a heavy drinker, but he wasn't neglectful or abusive. We did stuff as a family and he held down jobs. He was caring and attentive. He always took us swimming to the river Tisza. He didn't just go to the pub and stay there all the time – he was responsible, especially when he was a driving instructor.

My father started off as a nice alcoholic but his drinking got worse and worse. He became increasingly verbally and physically aggressive towards my mother, my younger brother and me. Then he lost his driving licence, so there was nothing to stop him from drinking full time.

My early childhood was uneventful, but it was broadly happy.

Me & my brother being happy and enjoying life

You know kids, when I was growing up we had a lots of bullies around the part of Szeged where we lived, called

Tarján district. It was a new development and I don't know what was there before but I know that there were a lots of gypsies.

The first bully in my life was a gypsy kid who terrorised not only me but almost every kid of my age. He was about 4–5 years older than us but he wasn't a big guy. He was only stronger than us because of his age. He actually was small for his age and that was why he picked on us. Within his age group he was probably a nobody or he was the one other kids bullied.

Once my father saw from our window that he was fighting with me, so he jumped out of the window, caught the kid and slapped him around. Of course, at that time it was allowed in Hungary. Nobody cared, especially, if it was an arsehole like this kid.

Anyway, as we were growing up, some of us got bigger and stronger than this little piece of shit, so we decided to take revenge on him because of the previous beatings he had inflicted on us. I volunteered to confront him because he was still stronger and bigger than me so I knew he would not back down from the fight. Then, the plan was that the other two friends of mine would come to help me and together we would beat him up this time.

The plan started out perfectly. We found him riding his bicycle and I put a stick through the wheel so he flew off of it. We had him where we wanted and he was furious. As soon as he had pulled himself together after his 'accident' he charged towards me. I was so proud of myself, I was even smiling, knowing that this time he was going to get it. Unfortunately, as he was running closer and closer towards me, my friends were getting further and further away from me. I started to think that our plan was probably not going to end up the way I had hoped. And I was right, kids. I was smaller and weaker but I wasn't a coward. I had picked the fight, so I stood my ground. As you guessed kids, I didn't last long.

When the gypsy kid left, I asked my friends 'What a fuck happened guys? Now I have a black eye or two, my nose is bleeding like it's never going to stop and my lips are torn apart so badly that I'm not going to be able to eat solid food for a week, while you guys were just watching. The plan wasn't for me to entertain you guys. Where the fuck were you? You were supposed to help me to beat the kid up not watch how he beats me up'. You know kids what they said? 'We got scared'. Good times, good times.

It wasn't the only time when my 'team' didn't back me up. But I still stood up every time and I still stand up every time for myself and for my friends' rights, even if it means that I'll be beaten up.

When I was a teenager there was another gypsy kid bullying everybody. On 1st May, we have a huge celebration in Hungary because of the International Workers' Day. We have parades and parties all over town – lots of people everywhere eating, drinking and having fun.

On one 1st May, a friend of mine yelled into the crowd: 'Sheep'. The crowd marched like a herd of sheep just as politically, most of the Hungarians acted like sheep.

Unfortunately, this gypsy bully had almost white hair and he thought that we were mocking him, so he came up to us and asked 'Are you talking to me?' I stood up again and told him 'No, we are not talking to you but what if we were? We are ten against you. What are you going to do?' Good guess kids, good guess again. He punched me in the face so hard that I passed out.

When I came around I asked the others, 'Did we beat him? Did we win?' Then they told me that after he knocked me out everybody shit their pants and did nothing. Another joyful moment of my life.

In my teens, I started to go off the rails. Not in my own eyes, of course, but my father became increasingly disapproving of everything I did.

By the third year of Vocational High School of Building and Construction, when I was 17, I started really hating it and neglected my studies in favour of going out partying and hanging around with groups of punks as well as actual underground punk groups. I dropped out of school altogether after that.

'Rocker' was the first fashion that really grabbed me – skinny jeans, denim jackets, boots like Dr Martens (we didn't have actual Dr Martens at that time), and I started listening to rock music – mostly Hungarian – because the authorities didn't want us to be exposed to decadent freedom music from outside the country. They thought it would corrupt the youth and make them want to overthrow the government. Idiots!

Then I moved onto the harder stuff – illegal underground Hungarian skinhead and punk bands and I spent a lots of my time hanging out with them. Bands like Boldog Idők (Happy Times) – actually they played ska music, 88 (Szeged's best skinhead group) and CPg (Come on Punk Group – 'definitely not as some detractors would have it, Cigány Pusztitó Gárda – Gypsy Extermination Guards').

CPg was formed in 1979 in Szeged by guitarist Zoltán 'Güzü' Benkő and Róbert Kövesi 'Boy'. Drummer Zoltán 'Kutyás' Nagy, vocalist Béla Haska and replacement bassist Zoltán 'Takony' Varga joined in 1981. They were notorious for their controversial stage antics and songs which openly criticised the Hungarian socialist government. Also, three of the band members were called Zoltán!

By the time I discovered them, they had already been banned from many local venues and they were forced to relocate to Budapest in 1982. Undeterred, I travelled on the train to Budapest many times to see them and other punk groups perform.

They did their final show on 5th March, 1983. Singer, Béla Haska brought a chicken on stage and ripped it apart. Because of that but mostly because of their lyrics against everything Hungary stood for all four members of the band were arrested for political agitation. After a six-month showcase trial, Güzü, Haska and Kutyás each received two-year jail sentences for anti-communist activity and Takony was placed on four year probation as a juvenile.

I got to know Güzü properly after he came out of prison and that's when we formed a lifelong friendship. He left Hungary and he went to Austria and the USA. He was living in New York and I met up with him in Santa Ana, California (a mutual friend of ours used to live there and we visited him at the same time) and in the same year he went back to Hungary. He was married but got divorced before he left the USA. In Hungary he had three kids from three girlfriends so I beat him by the number of kids but not by the number of their mothers. Anyway, the band reformed in the late nineties and it is still performing today.

We went to Budapest many times for gigs, and band members and other skinhead and punk friends would come from Budapest to visit us in Szeged. We were fed and always found a floor to sleep on in Budapest and we returned the hospitality back home, but we had to sneak guests into the flat without my father finding out.

We had a ground-floor balcony and there was a little 'half-room' between my parents' bedroom and mine, so if we were quiet, we could manage it. My mother never had a problem with any of my friends; she cooked for them and made them breakfast, but if we ever woke my father up, he called the police.

The Hungarian government hated these skinhead and punk groups because they thought they were planning revolution, but we were planning nothing. We just wanted to have a good time. If we met up it wasn't to plot to overthrow the government, it was to party and have fun and listen to music. My favourite Western skinhead and punk bands were and are The Toy Dolls (I saw them perform in Szeged), The 4-Skins, the Böhse Onkelz, the Ramones (I saw them perform 3–4 times in Toronto) and the Sex Pistols, but my favourite music is Ska music – Madness, The Specials, Bad Manners, The Beat, The Selector (I saw all of them performing in different cities and countries). I longed to live in the UK.

CHAPTER FOUR

BEAT ON THE BRAT

From the age of fifteen until August 1986 when I was forced to join the military, aged 19, I was out partying with the underground skinhead and punk groups and going to parties where that kind of music was played. But it wasn't a violent scene. For example, there was no animosity between skinheads and punks, like in the UK.

Unsurprisingly, my lifestyle frequently attracted the attention of the local police, who were mostly corrupt and violent bullies. When I was young I got beaten up many times by the police, mostly for no reason. If I had long hair then I was a punk, if I had short hair then I was a skinhead, but I even got beaten up just because I was chewing gum. The police would beat up non-conformist teens like me on a whim.

I didn't have any role models because there was no one I could look up to. Everywhere I went I was an outsider, but I was sick of playing by the rules. Not even my father protected me. My mother was very supportive. She loved everyone, even my scariest looking friends but they were just harmless teen rebels. I loved skinhead and punk music and the anti-establishment attitude and I liked the look on others, but actually I didn't go skinhead then or full punk with spiky hair and safety pins.

When I went to parties, I'd get drunk but I wasn't smoking weed – yet. But we did experiment with other things: I'd stolen a pad of prescriptions from the old people's home where my mother worked, so we had access to a lots of illicit opium-based prescription medication. Which was nice!

Also, at that time, fields of opium poppies grew in abundance in Hungary (not any more). Back then, you could harvest your own poppies, cut the heads off and brew a crude, vile tasting tea that produced an opiate high.

Later, we learned how to cut the heads properly, gather the milky liquid and cook it (I didn't know how to cook it and still don't know) and that became heroin that we could inject. Several of my friends became addicted and unfortunately some died. I injected our homemade heroin a few times but thankfully I never got addicted or inadvertently overdosed.

I was happy being a harmless delinquent, but my dad hated me more and more. It wasn't long before he despised everything that I represented.

Bear & me getting ready for the night

These young punk guys I called friends were already on the blacklist with the police, they were driving around all over town in their unmarked police cars and they would chase us if they saw us. If they caught us somehow, and you were with us, you were put on the blacklist too, even if you didn't do anything.

They could put you on the blacklist for any reason, and beat you up for nothing. On one end of my street was the school and the other end was the police station. I made the mistake once of trying to sneak past the police station and as soon as they saw me through the window they ran out and they caught me, they dragged me into the police station beat me up and demanded I confess what I was planning against the government.

I told them I wasn't planning anything, but they said they knew I was in that group – that they had caught me with them many times, and they were convinced that they were planning something which I had to tell them. Then they beat me up again.

I was just hanging out, like a lots of teenagers, not really doing anything wrong apart from being with the 'wrong' crowd. But I definitely wanted nothing to do with the adult world I saw around me – drones getting up and going to work, every day. They were grey and boring and miserable.

They looked sad compared to people in England. They always complained, had sad stories, but they still obediently went to work and did what was expected of them. They were not happy – but I was happy and they hated that. I could be laughing and making jokes with my friends and sometimes we'd get attacked in the street just for being happy.

One time we sat on the bus together with a bunch of lifeless workers going to work. We'd been out partying all night and still having fun – you should have seen the hatred in their eyes just because of that.

There were restrictions on everything. Everyone had to have work; it was mandatory. If you didn't have work for 30 days, the police could lock you up for 30 days. If you lost your job, then you had to find another one quickly.

The next time you were caught without a job, it was 60 days in prison, then 90 days, and so on, just because you didn't work. So we always tried to find some shitty job even if it only lasted a week, and then the 30 days' grace started again after that. You weren't helped to get a job, but there was plenty of work, very shitty jobs that always needed filling.

My first & last Hungarian ID at age 14

We all had to carry ID cards – a little booklet that was full of personal information, including name, photo, address, birthplace, employment history and current place of work.

Until the age of eighteen, your parents could vouch for you and say they were supporting you and giving you food and board, but once you turned 18, parental protection was not allowed, so you had to work.

We also had to endure 'Communist Saturday'. This meant that on those Saturdays, everybody had to go to work, but the money we earned went to 'build the communism'. We didn't get paid for that day. It wasn't enough earning shitty money even if we got paid, you had to work for free too here and there. That 'building the communism' bullshit was just ridiculous. All the money we earned that day went into the pockets of the 'fearless leaders'.

Besides 'Communist Saturday', all school children had to work for free on government farms, picking grapes, apples or other fruit for two weeks every year. Imagine that kids! We had no school for that fortnight but instead we had to work very hard. Of course, it was mandatory. I hated that, so every time I just took it slowly and did as little as possible. There was a reward for whoever picked the most but it was only a 'well done' written in our booklet by the head teacher, so who in their right mind gave a fuck?

We had to team up in pairs and work all day. The teachers kept count of how many buckets of apples or boxes of grapes we collected. Even though we worked in pairs, we were evaluated as individuals. So the first bucket or box was marked to one of a pair and the second to the other person and so on. Because of this system, I was the one with the lowest mark many times. But once, I only picked three boxes of grapes all day and my buddy picked four. The next lowest after us picked 18 boxes. Up until then, there had been a reward for the best only and nothing for the worst but because this time there was such a difference between me and the next lowest (not counting my buddy), the head teacher wrote a warning in my booklet. What the fuck? What was I, a child slave? Of course I complained because we were working in pairs so it meant that I picked just as much as my buddy but the head teacher didn't care.

I'm not sure if I mentioned it earlier, but hardly any teachers liked me. Actually, hardly any adults liked me. I have a big mouth they said. It wasn't true. I was only standing up for myself. I fought against injustice and I still do.

We also had 'Building Camps' for two weeks in the summer. It wasn't mandatory and we got paid for it. I only went once with my best friends Lacika and Ofi. There were lots of other friends from my neighbourhood and most of us went to the same school too. The work sucked but I lost my virginity there. Let me tell you kids how it went.

The camp started in July 1984 during a very hot summer. Our job was detasseling corn (removing the pollen-producing tassel to prevent self-fertilisation). Corn plants have very sharp leaves, so we had to wear protective clothing, which consisted of a pair of wellies, plastic trousers and yellow jacket. So kids, imagine a hot summer, you are in a corn field without any shade and working hard, wearing only plastic clothing. Are we thinking the same thing – torture? The elasticated cuffs of our plastic jackets clung tightly to our wrists. After working an hour in these conditions, when we loosened our cuffs, a litre of sweat would pour out. OK, we had breaks every few hours but it was still unbearable.

We started 8:00am, had lunch at noon and finished working at 5:00pm. After work we returned to the camp, showered and had dinner at 7:00pm. Only after dinner were we allowed to have some fun. Luckily, it was a mixed-sex camp so we could impress the 'ladies'. We had different kind of activities and campfires at the end of each day. Lights out was at 10:00pm. Boys and girls had separate barracks and nobody was allowed to leave the barracks after 10:00pm unless they needed the loo.

The camp was policed by the teachers. They had to make sure that everybody went to work and returned safely, that we didn't bring any alcohol or cigarettes into the camp, that we behaved nicely and – most important of all – that boys and girls didn't mix in the barracks after lights out. But that didn't stop us. We had alcohol and cigarettes and we mixed with the girls.

Nothing much happened for the first few nights, we just talked in the barracks and then went to sleep. But one night, we heard girls calling our names from the nearby barrack: 'Zoltán Mihály, Lacika, come over'. And again: 'Zoltán Mihály, Lacika, come over'. And again, and again, and again that siren call. Lacika wanted to go after the first call but I had a girlfriend back in Szeged and I loved her very much. Besides, we didn't know who was calling us. They could have been ugly. Not that it mattered at that age. We just wanted to have sex. Looks didn't come into it. On the other hand, my girlfriend Tündike was a very nice looking girl with a great personality and I loved her. Many guys wanted to be with her but she chose me. Don't ask me why because I don't know. She was from a wealthy family. I don't know what her father did for a job, but they lived in a huge house in Újszeged (the other side of river Tisza where mostly wealthy people lived). Her mother looked like a trophy wife, she was just as beautiful as Tündike. Tündike's mother was always nice to me and even liked my jokes. I wasn't even banned from being home alone with Tündike (until then I had only been allowed to visit my girlfriends when the parents were home). I was allowed to go up to Tündike's room and close the door. They were a very nice family but of course I screwed that up too. Tündike wasn't ready for sex yet. We did stuff, but there was no actual sex. Anyway, the girls were still calling us and Lacika wouldn't let up.

In those days we didn't need protection from STDs but there was a contraceptive pill that the girls could take one hour after sex but I didn't have one. Naturally, Lacika had three, so it wasn't a problem. I had run out of excuses not to go, so I gave in and we sneaked into the girls' barracks.

We had bunk beds in the camp and the two girls who had been calling us shared one, so Lacika took the bottom one and I went to the top. I'm not sure how much my girl enjoyed the sex because I was done in five minutes or maybe fewer but that's how it works at a young age. But, as my friend told a girl who complained: 'Darling, you had the same amount of time as me'. My girl didn't complain but she told me, after sex, that she wanted to be with Lacika and that the other girl wanted to be with me. Then I wondered: are girls just like boys? Didn't it matter who they were with as long as it was a boy? Anyway, she took the pill and we said 'goodbye' but before I could leave she asked me to come back the next night. So I couldn't have been that bad. I didn't have any pills so I had to ask Lacika to give me his last one and as my best friend and wingman, he gave it to me.

The next day, I wrote to my brother to ask him to send me more pills. I visited the girl the next night too and luckily, my brother's pills arrived within three days. The only problem was that sex was forbidden in the camp and when letters arrived the teachers checked them for 'contraband'. They easily felt the pills through the envelope, so it was bye bye sex.

The teachers told me I had one more strike and then they would kick me out. This conversation took place in front of the whole camp so everybody could hear and learn from it. Many of us didn't want to stay in the camp anyway because a few days earlier we had found out how little money we would be getting for this horrible job but we didn't know how to quit. So I told the teachers: 'This place is like a concentration camp. We work our arses off for almost nothing and now you take away the only joy we have'. The teachers told me to sit down and be quiet or they would kick me out so I told them: 'You don't have to kick me out. Just give me my fucking pills back and

I'm leaving'. Of course, they didn't give me my pills back but they asked if anyone else felt the same way about the camp. Some of my friends stood up and so we all went packing. Szeged wasn't far so we hopped on the bus and we were home within an hour or so. The problem was that my friend Ofi didn't want his parents know that he had quit, so he asked if he could crash at my place until camp had ended. 'Of course', I said but now there was another problem. Ofi lived in next but one building to me so we had to be very careful to avoid running into his parents but somehow we managed it.

As honest as I am, I told Tündike what had happened at the camp and she broke up with me. I don't blame her but it still broke my heart. The girl from the camp became my sex partner (not girlfriend). She wasn't the best looking girl and after a while I visited her less and less. Once we ran in to each other at a party when I was drunk and we had sex. She soon spotted that I was more interested in her when I was drunk so from then on, every time she invited me to her flat she always bought a bottle of vermouth. The more I drank, the more attractive she became and we would have sex. But after a while not even the vermouth was enough so I just told her that I didn't want to see her any more.

CHAPTER FIVE

SOMEBODY PUT SOMETHING IN MY DRINK

So now I was 18, I had to hold down a job without going nuts, so after doing lots of shitty ones, my friend Skin and I decided we would become sailors – not on the high seas but on rivers.

Nevertheless, we had to go through some medical examinations and we had to swim a certain distance and then we got the certificate what we had to provide when we were applying for a sailor position. That could only be done in Budapest, so we caught a train there and completed the application process.

After that we visited Skin's friends in Budapest. I didn't know those guys. They were all skinheads. At that time I had nice long hair, not too long, but longer than the skinheads. After introductions we started drinking, listening to music and talking.

Everything was fine until we got shit-faced. Then a few of the guys decided that I had to become a skinhead as well. I didn't agree with them, but they were very insistent. So I tried to placate them whilst remaining cool:

'Nah, it doesn't really matter' I said, casually, 'I like my hair. I like your music. I like you guys. You know, I have no problem with you at all, but I don't want to have short hair'.

They wouldn't take no for an answer and the atmosphere started to get tense. I didn't know anyone else in the room, apart from Skin, who was no help because for some reason he wasn't around. Eventually, a skinhead called Árpi told the rest of them to all 'shut the fuck up' and leave me alone.

After that, they were fine with my hair. Suddenly they didn't want to cut it after all. I didn't know then but Árpi had quite a reputation as a tough guy amongst the skinhead population in Hungary. Even Hungarian skinhead groups like Egészséges Fejbőr (Healthy Headskin) sang songs about him. After this incident, the whole night went back to being solely about drinking, listening to music and talking.

By the end of the night I was passing-out drunk. I didn't know anybody, so I had no place to sleep. But I was so drunk, I didn't care. The usual protocol in such situations was if you are so drunk that you are not sure how you are going to get home, just have a few more drinks and you'll wake up at home.

But I was in Budapest and not in my home town. So I knew the routine, which was that if someone came up from Szeged to Budapest, they went to someone's place to sleep. And if someone came down from Budapest to Szeged, it was the same thing.

The next morning I woke up in a strange room, with a blackout memory of how I'd got there – so no memory whatsoever. Inside my mouth, my dry tongue felt like a dead planet. My head was throbbing as if I had taken a police-beating.

I looked around. There was just me in the room. I was sleeping on the floor. There was an empty bed beside me. I didn't even know what happened. But I was alive. How had I got here? I needed the loo, so I staggered out of the room into a small kitchen, where I encountered a family eating breakfast.

'Hello, I'm Zoltán. Pleased to meet you'. I tried to sound as polite, sober and respectable as possible, which was a challenge, as I realised that I was only wearing a T-

Shirt and my underwear. I quickly scanned the faces – father, mother, sister – to see if I recognised anyone from the previous evening, but I drew a blank.

After a brief tense silence, which seemed to last forever, the mother smiled and spoke quietly: 'My son has gone to buy some cigarettes but he will be back soon. Please make yourself at home. Would you like some tea?'

'Yes, thank you. I'll just . . . get . . . myself ready'. Cringing inwardly, I tiptoed politely away in my socks, went to the toilet, dressed quickly and sat down with the family to have breakfast. I still had no idea where I was or why I was here. In silence I busied myself politely buttering a small bread roll with an intense focus, raising my head occasionally to smile appreciatively at my hosts. Then I helped myself to a spoonful of jam, bit into the roll, nodded and forced a beaming smile. I swore to myself that I would never drink again.

Then Árpi appeared in the doorway. So I was in Árpi's house. Ah, the relief. Everyone in the room visibly relaxed. Luckily, he remembered what had happened the night before. So he mentioned that we got drunk and then Skin went to someone else's place and that we were going to meet up after breakfast.

After breakfast, we left the flat, met up with the others and after a few drinks, Skin and I travelled home to Szeged.

This story is all the more interesting to me because after that one occasion, I went to skinhead and punk gigs in Budapest several times during the following year, but never ran into Árpi again. Then I left Hungary and didn't think about or meet Árpi until I accidentally ran into him years later at a friend of a friend's place in Vienna, and it was only then that we became very good friends.

CHAPTER SEX

PUNISHMENT FITS THE CRIME

Once when I went to a concert in Szeged, Hungary, I'm not sure if it was to see the group called 88 or CPg, but I'm certain it was illegal. The police found out because they had informants within our circle of friends, so that was their probable source. The same thing happened many times before and after.

They raided the concert and demanded to see everybody's papers. When I gave them my papers, I was very drunk, so naturally I thought it would be hilarious to steal a policeman's hat and run away with it. So that's what I did.

Unfortunately, there was another group of people helping the police on this occasion because there were lots of kids in the concert and too few police to check everybody's papers and arrest them.

These people were like volunteer police. They couldn't do anything without the police, they were civilians but they could help the police and there were young fit guys amongst them.

I was drunk so I couldn't run very fast so they quickly caught up with me and then dragged me back to the club where the concert had been. They kept me there in the back garden area which had a very high fence and I expected they would hold me until everybody had been cleared to leave and then they could take me to the police station for a good beating.

So I was sitting there very drunk and wondering what was going to happen to me. I was certain they were going to beat me up again. Then I had another brilliant idea. Somehow I managed to climb over the huge fence and run home. I was very lucky that night.

I knew they're going to find me because they took my papers and my address was in it. But I was lucky because my papers said I was living with my grandma even though in real life I was living at home with my parents. It was only because of some inheritance fees. By living with her as a caregiver for a certain amount of years I wouldn't have to pay for inheriting my grandma's flat after she died, or something like that. I was too young to care about this kind of thing.

Anyhow, when the police came, of course, I wasn't there. Luckily, my grandma wasn't there either. So they just dropped my documents through to the letter box.

Maybe they were embarrassed that I had escaped and they didn't want to have any record of it. So they gave me my papers back without beating me up. And next time, when I went to my grandma, she returned them to me. I told her that I lost them somewhere and probably some honest guy found and returned it.

In England I didn't have to steel the policeman's hat, I just had to ask for it

It was kind of funny. We were talking about it for a long time and even nowadays when we get together, still laugh about it.

CHAPTER SEVEN

HERE TODAY, GONE TOMORROW

I was 19 when I left Hungary, but a year earlier my brother had escaped with my passport and I had helped some of my friends escape too. When my friends Szkuri and Doxen wanted to escape from Hungary to Traiskirchen, Austria, my friend Tigi and I escorted them to the railway station in Szeged to say goodbye, give them strength to carry out their plan and to support them emotionally. Of course, we were drinking and so we decided to go with them to Budapest and say goodbye there as they were boarding the train to Vienna.

The only problem was that we had neither a ticket nor money. Then we figured out that Tigi and I could lie under Szkuri and Doxen's seats and they would cover us with their feet and their luggage on the floor so that the conductor couldn't see us. So that's what we did.

We managed to avoid the first ticket check, but it was very uncomfortable under the seats; we were already numb, so there was no way we could hold out for an entire three-hour journey from Szeged to Budapest.

After the conductor walked past us the first time, we knew we had at least 20 minutes until his return, so Szkuri and Doxen, who had tickets, kept watch so we could sit normally and continue drinking until his next visit.

It wasn't long before we were shit-faced, so we didn't bother to hide again for the rest of the journey. We sat with Szkuri and Doxen, drinking comfortably on the seats. The conductor passed by several times, but either he thought he had checked our tickets already or he was just a nice guy, but he didn't bother us again.

It didn't matter to us, we were only interested in getting to Budapest in relative comfort so we could put Szkuri and Doxen on the train to Vienna and say goodbye to them in Budapest, which we managed without a hitch. Now all we had to do was get home, with no money.

The Viennese train departed from a different station in Budapest than the one to Szeged, so Tigi and I walked to the Nyugati (West) Railway Station, to catch the Szeged train.

We started to sober up, but since we didn't have any money, we decided to look for a shop where we could steal some alcohol. Luckily, we found one in a short time.

My friend Tigi was a very skilful and seasoned shoplifter. I wasn't at that stage (although that soon changed when I reached Vienna about a year later). We went into the store and looked around to see what kind of alcohol we could easily steal.

I distracted the shopkeeper while Tigi 'packed' (secreted alcohol under his coat). Luckily, there were canned beers near the door, which were very rare and expensive in Hungary at that time. I don't even remember drinking it before then. Tigi packed a 24 pack and we made a quick exit.

A few minutes later, we were walking to the train station, drinking the well-deserved fruits of our labour and feeling smug that we had experienced the luxury of these canned beers before Szkuri and Doxen.

We didn't have money to buy tickets, but we were so drunk that we didn't care. We boarded the train home to Szeged, thinking we would avoid the conductor again.

Unfortunately, just before we reached Cegléd, which is about a third of the way to Szeged, we spotted the conductor in the next carriage. There was nowhere to run or hide. Luckily a plan formed in our drunken heads. We figured, if we climbed out the door of the speeding train and clung on either side of it using the hand rails and then shut the door, we would be hidden from sight and the conductor would be none the wiser. Then we would simply climb back into the carriage when she was gone.

Everything went well but we were so drunk that we didn't notice that the conductor had actually already spotted us earlier. We had climbed out and were clinging onto the handrails, congratulating ourselves for our genius plan, when her head appeared out of the window.

She shouted and swore at us for our dangerous stupidity and of course, the police were already waiting for us at the Cegléd station when we arrived and were forced to leave the train.

They asked for our papers and wrote down our details. The truth is, I have no idea if we were fined or not, but they certainly waited until the train left so we wouldn't get back on it and then they let us go because our papers were in order.

The next train to Szeged wasn't for hours and we were hungry after drinking so much, so we found a store nearby and stole some food. Unfortunately, I was too drunk to steal but Tigi was luckier – he scored a tin of lunch meat, although I managed to cut my hand whilst attempting to open it.

At the station, we waited for the next Szeged train to arrive from Budapest and jumped on board just before it departed. After drinking the rest of the beers, we fell asleep and woke up in Szeged.

So that was my first adventure with Tigi, which cemented our friendship. Before long he became one of my best friends and we shared lots of adventures together in several western countries, after we both fled from Hungary.

CHAPTER EIGHT

MENTAL HELL

Military service was still mandatory at the time. I was not supposed to go into the army for another year, but this was where my father stepped in and interfered. He did some driving for the Hungarian military so he had connections and made sure that I was sent into military service as soon as possible.

On Saturday 23rd August 1986, I returned home after a three-day party to find a letter waiting for me, an 'invitation' to enlist on the Monday. The army deliberately left me little time to prepare because I think they were afraid that I would find a way to avoid it. And they were right.

Under normal circumstances, the 'invitation' is usually sent out a month before enlistment day and I should have been enlisted a year later anyway. When someone was past 18 years old, they were called in for an interview and some tests. This consisted of various medical, psychological and physical examinations and these determined what position the person would be given in the military and when he should enlist in the army.

Good athletes went into the sports military unit, masons and architects into the construction unit, anyone with a truck license got to drive trucks in the military. I was enlisted as a diver when I was 18 but under normal circumstances, I shouldn't have been called up until I was 20.

The military also employed civilians and so my father worked for them as a chauffeur. He was a driver for some high-ranking military officer for years. My father despised my attitude and life choices, so he contacted this particular military officer and arranged for me to enlist me a year earlier as a soldier and to post me as far away from Szeged as possible and without any friends. So that's the way it happened.

My father wanted me to have the worst time of my life. I didn't hate him for that, he was my father so I liked him as a father but hated him as a person all the same. Actually, at the time I didn't realise that it was his doing, he only admitted it to me many years later, but he still thought he had done the right thing. He hadn't really achieved much in his life, but he wanted me to be like him. Maybe he wanted me to achieve more than him.

To avoid the hundreds of young people coming from Szeged and its surroundings, I was sent alone to a place called Börgönd. I didn't even know where it was. The others were placed in groups of 20 and 30 for various military units and they were escorted to the appropriate place. Since I was heading to Börgönd alone, I didn't even get an escort.

But to return to the Saturday before my entry: as soon as I learned that I had to enlist in a few days, I hastily fabricated an escape plan. The old people's home in Szeged where my mother worked, was about a 10-minute walk from our flat, so I decided I would stage a fake suicide attempt.

Since my mother had the key to the safe at work, my plan was that she could pretend to forget the key and therefore 'unexpectedly' have to come home for it. By the time she got home, I would have taken a lots of different kind of prescription drugs, like I wanted to commit suicide and then just stretch out on the bed.

When my mother arrived home 'unexpectedly' and

found me lying on the bed she would call the ambulance. I was taking pills as a drug anyway, so I knew what dosage would only make me dizzy, light-headed, shaky and weak without actually killing me.

On the other hand, I would have to put a bunch of empty medicine boxes on the bed too to make my situation look even more serious. I also knew that those who commit suicide are not released from hospital until they sign a statement that they no longer a danger to themselves.

I was fully prepared to wait in the hospital for a few weeks to avoid the enlistment and then sign the release statement afterwards. Then, by the next enlistment date, I would have left the country and gone to Italy to meet my brother.

Of course, my mum was too honest to be involved in this plan so I had to abandon it. There was nothing to be done, except drink and have fun for the remaining two days with my friend Rubber, who actually, slept at my place on the Sunday night so he could escort me on Monday morning.

On Monday morning, my parents and Rubber and I left for the Szeged Sports Stadium, where the gathering was. I discussed with my friend Rubber that he would get some vodka and I would slip out of the stadium to meet him as soon as I could. Once inside the sports hall, we had to go for either a medical examination or a personal briefing, I don't remember which, but I was able to slip away easily.

About ten people had to go at once and while one person was called in, the others waited in the hallway. I knew the stadium well, so escaping was no problem. My friend Rubber and I drank the vodka and said goodbye to each other.

I gave him my 'small passport' so he could escape from Hungary. I assumed we wouldn't be meeting again for a long time. This passport was good to enter the former

Yugoslavia only.

A huge part of Yugoslavia belonged to Hungary for a long time, so after the First World War, when the land was divided up, families were separated. So there were two kinds of passports – one was a general passport, the other 'small' one was just for 30km within Yugoslavia.

Over the last year, a very close friendship had developed between Rubber and me. Even today, I consider him one of my best friends, even though we haven't seen each other in years. Regardless, I still think a lot about him and I hope he does the same too. Every time I think of him I remember the good old days when nothing was more important than having fun. Since none of us worked, we weren't really able to come up with the things we needed to have fun so we stole everything.

We spent almost all our time on the street, we hardly went home to sleep. That is why we stole not only alcohol but also food. After I got enlisted, we knew that we would not see each other much in the next 18 months (because that's how long the military was at the time), so we had partied even harder in the final days before my enrolment.

I remember one night I woke up to someone kicking me. I looked up and saw another figure kicking my friend Rubber in a similar style and yelling: 'Are you animals? You sleeping here right in the middle of the bridge? Anyone can run you over!'

We gained consciousness very quickly because of all the kicking and yelling. Then we saw that we were indeed on the bridge in the middle of the road and the two figures disturbing our dreams were two detectives whom we knew quite well and unfortunately, they knew us too.

One of them started yelling at me: 'Mihály, it's you again? You're lucky this time because in a few days you have to enlist in the military. Go home and I don't want to see you again before your enlistment. The military will make you a man'.

Before we had passed out, we had just stolen some grapes, but since they weren't sweet enough, we started throwing them at each other and when that got boring, we just crushed them all over our faces. We squashed them in each other's hair and clothes.

By the time the detectives found us the grape juice had dried, leaving our clothes and hair crusty and brittle. We were sticky and stinking badly. Rubber lived closer, so we went to his flat to sleep. We didn't bother to take a shower; we just collapsed into sleep again with our dirty clothes on. In those days, such things did not bother me at all.

But let's go back to the stadium. Feeling sad, I sneaked back to the hallway where I had been told to wait, but by then no one was there. There was already a full search in progress for me. I lied and pretended I was still drunk from the previous night's farewell party and had fallen asleep on the toilet. After arranging everything I needed, I set off for Börgönd alone.

In the stadium, they told me how to get to Börgönd, so at least I knew the route: Szeged – Budapest – Székesfehérvár – Börgönd. Sometime in the afternoon I got to Budapest and I was already very hungry, so I bought a hamburger. Of course, by the time I'd eaten it, I'd managed to miss the connection to Székesfehérvár so I had to wait hours for the next train.

All the new enlisted people have to get to their units by midnight, but since I missed my connection in Budapest, it was already past midnight and I was still on the train to Börgönd. I didn't know where to get off, so I asked the conductor to tell me when it was time.

After a while, he said: 'We're here'. I opened the door and could only see a huge wilderness an endless field.

'Are you sure this is the right place?' I asked the guard. 'Yes,' he replied, 'just go to the other end of the field and you'll see the military barracks'. He was telling the truth.

It was a long walk, but I got there in the end.

Everyone already suspected I wasn't coming because the last person had arrived hours earlier. By then, all the other recruits had had their hair cut short and had been issued with their military uniform, boots and other accoutrements. By the time I arrived, everything was locked up, so I was told to go to sleep and that I would be sorted the next morning.

In the morning I was able to view the small grim military base in daylight. We were in the middle of nowhere, surrounded by farming fields and in the distance leading to the horizon were more fields. The entire area was very flat. At least that meant they couldn't send us on exhausting mountain training. There were several dismal identical mustard-coloured concrete barracks, four storeys high with flat roofs, which looked like modern student accommodation, only bleaker and shabbier. I remember that all the window frames were painted grey. There was one taller four-storey building which looked like a farmhouse, with four rows of five windows and a gable roof – which was also a barrack. There were also a couple of large hangars, with large sliding doors made out of vertical wooden slats below a lattice of windows and a corrugated metal roof.

During the first few days, there were only briefings on life in the army, barracks and units rules and various other regulations, so somehow my haircut and military uniform were overlooked. For three days I marched alongside my fellow soldiers with long hair and wearing civilian clothing. Then suddenly a high-ranking military officer (to this day I don't know military ranks or recognise them from their military uniform) came over to me and balled me out: 'Just who do you think you are? You're in the army now son, not living in a filthy squat in Budapest. Why haven't you cut your hair and where is your uniform? You're a disgrace to yourself and to your unit—'

'It's not my fault!' I yelled back at him, my spine tingling with excitement at just how much shit I was getting myself into, not only talking back to a senior officer but shouting in his face. I felt a bit lightheaded, as though I might pass out. I thought I was such a brave anti-hero but I must have looked like a complete knob head but you know kids, I never liked rules or obey them. I fully expected to be 'court-martialled' on the spot or at the very least smashed in the chin with the butt of a rifle, like in the movies, but for some reason the senior officer turned purple, spun sharply around and started barking orders at the soldier who was in charge of us: 'Captain, take this miserable specimen to the barber immediately and give him a buzz cut, pronto, top priority. You can tell him on whose orders you are acting. Off you go'.

Árpi's friends couldn't make me a skinhead, but the military did. I stared wistfully at myself in the mirror as the barber roughly shaved my head, giving me a 'Number 2'. There were none of the niceties you'd expect from a barber, no black polyester cape to cover my torso, just my naked upper body; no talcum powder on the back of the neck, no mirror at the end to show the back of the head. The guy may as well have been shearing a sheep. After he'd finished turning me into a number, I collected my military uniform and everything else I needed. I finally looked like a soldier. The resemblance ended there.

Compared to the lifestyle I had before, it was hell. From the first day, an idiot came into our barrack at 5:30am and started yelling, 'Comrades wake up!'. It was so annoying that I think I was up at 5:20am on the third day just to avoid being woken by this moron yelling.

The food was awful. There was no hot water. We had to shower in cold water and then run around a flat field ad nauseam in the name of basic training. After a few days, I started hiding in the toilet block to avoid the running.

Most of the guys couldn't even write. I had nothing in

common with them. I couldn't talk to them about anything. Several asked me to write their letters for them because I could spell and write legibly and my letters were readable and meaningful (the military read every letter we sent or received).

I was supposed to endure 18 months of this. There was no way I was going to do that. I had a free life before I enlisted. I hung out with friends, drank, took drugs. We were having fun and we didn't care about the world. We usually went to bed at dawn and only 'recovered' in the afternoon and continued where we had previously left off. I resolved that as soon as they let us go home on our first leave, I would go AWOL.

All the soldiers who had enlisted before us were our superiors, so we had to do whatever they said without question. We were once assigned to clean their barracks. Of course, no one liked me because I was an urban kid and completely different from them, so I was given the toilet cleaning job.

The cleaning chemical had a very toxic fume so no one should work with it for more than 30–40 minutes. Of course, they forgot about me and by the time they remembered it was an hour and a half later and I already was blue and green.

They were very scared so they quickly stopped me and invited me to their common room to watch TV and offered me all kinds of food delicacies that had been sent to them from home. The others were taken back to our barracks and everyone was looking for me. Meanwhile, I was having a nice meal comfortably sitting in the front of the telly.

A few hours later, someone remembered to ask the 'old' soldiers if they had seen me and that's how they found me. All these things and the fact that Börgönd was one day's train ride away from Szeged, all hardened my resolve to run away as soon as I had made my military oath.

We completed basic training in a month and then we got our first leave. This was my chance to escape.

CHAPTER NINE

TAKE THE PAIN AWAY

The ringing of the clock stopped me dreaming and woke me up in a matter of moments. I began to recover nicely, slowly, but before I could reach a state of full vigilance, I noticed that I had a really bad hangover. So what was new?

My head was spinning, nausea appeared, and knowing what day was ahead of me, I wished I was dead because I hasn't said no to the party the night before. For the past few years, I have been drinking and using drugs like it was my sacred calling.

It's true that it didn't pay, but at least I didn't have to pay for it either. So I wouldn't stop for any money. I passed out three or four times a week and when I gained consciousness I had no idea what had happened to me the night before.

It was a little confusing at first, but every 'calling' has its drawbacks. I didn't know much about these disadvantages at the time, as I not only didn't like to work, I didn't even work. As I told you kids, in the old socialist Hungary, not having a job was punishable, so I had to feel good every day in a bit of fear but I can proudly say, I succeeded very well in light of the circumstances.

Let's get back to my current condition, which was pretty woeful. I had a hard time getting out of bed and getting dressed. I tried to move as slowly as possible, but it still felt like a sharp arrow entered into my brain at every minute. I felt like it wanted to explode.

My first trip this morning led to one of my best friends Rubber. Before I enlisted as a soldier, I had given him my 'small passport'. After I came home on leave, I discovered that he hadn't left the country after all, so I needed to get my passport back from him.

I paid Rubber a visit. Fortunately, he was home. I told him how awful the military was: the early mornings, the heinous food, the morons I had to put up with every day, not a drop of hot water and I'm sure I told him another thousand reasons why I didn't want to go back and waste my time in the army.

He gave me back my passport and I told him my plan. He was the only person who knew about it and who also helped me. The help was to escorting me everywhere I had to go to be able to leave the country. To do this, we first had to go to the bank and redeem the required amount of dinars (300 dinars was mandatory, no more, no less), and then we bought my bus ticket to Subotica in the former Yugoslavia (now in Serbia).

My bus left at 10:00am and since we had arranged everything and I still had an hour, we sat in a nearby boozer for a few beers. We didn't talk much, even though we knew we wouldn't meet much in the near future. When it was finally time for me to leave, we hugged goodbye and I boarded the bus.

I crossed the border without any problems. I couldn't take much stuff with me otherwise it would have raised suspicions. When I reached Subotica, I phoned my brother, who was living in Italy. I told him that I had deserted from the Hungarian military and fled Hungary and I asked him to come and meet me.

As you know kids, my brother had left Hungary the year before. He was only 17 at that time. He couldn't get his passport approved (the work place had to approve the passport application at that time), but I already had a passport because I'd applied for one when I was sixteen. So I had a passport already and I gave it to him. We looked so similar that people would frequently mistake us for each other around the town. He was shorter than me and I was skinner and taller, but our faces looked alike and on a passport you only see a face.

He went to Austria but told them his real age of 17, so they told him he was too young to stay, so he went to Italy. Since he couldn't use my passport to meet me (because he had to give it up when he registered as a political refugee), he had to cross the border without it. We agreed to go to Belgrade train station and wait for each other every couple of hours from 6:00pm on Wednesday night, which was two days later.

This was it, I couldn't go back because I knew that I would have to face a prison sentence and as it turned out, in my absence I was tried by a military court and sentenced to ten years for going AWOL. Actually my brother also would have faced three years in prison for fleeing Hungary without permission and with my passport. So we were both wanted men with a strong incentive not to get caught.

My brother was almost convicted too, for beating up a guy but luckily he left Hungary before the police caught up with him. We were having a night out just like any other. We went from boozer to boozer and when we ran out of money, we just stole a few bottles of vodka and continued our night on the street. Now, earlier I told you about the 'volunteer police' who helped when the police force by itself just wasn't enough, like illegal concerts. They had no authority without police present but some of these guys thought that they were already the police and had the same authority.

One of these arseholes came up to us and started giving us orders, thinking that we would be afraid of him. We hardly took orders from the police, let alone this idiot, but we were polite to him at first: we told him to 'fuck off'. But as you guessed, he didn't listen, so my brother kicked his teeth in so hard, he was probably shitting them out for days.

I didn't recognise him but unfortunately, he remembered me because a few weeks earlier we had interviewed for the military on the same day. On that day, only recruits with a surname starting with an M were there and while we were arguing I called my brother 'brother', so that was enough information for the police to search for me. I guess their search got easier as soon as they found my name among those who were on the military interview the same day as this moron. I doubt they searched any further, since my brother and I were both on the police's 'blacklist' and because only a few weeks later, I received an 'invitation' from the police for an 'interview'.

I had totally forgotten about this incident because at that time in Hungary, normally no one ran to the police because of a little punch in the face. I was well acquainted with getting 'invitations' from the police which meant a little talk and a big beating but I still went to find out why they wanted to beat me up. When I was young, I must have been a curious wee fella.

At the police station they put me in the 'lineup' (I was the only one in it) and the idiot made a positive identification that I was only the brother of the suspect. Then they questioned me about the incident and my brother's involvement in it. Luckily, my brother was already in Italy so I had no reason to lie and provoke an unnecessary beating from the police, so I told them everything. I also told them that my brother was in Italy and wasn't coming back so they couldn't take the case any further. They told me they would have to close it. I was free to go without a beating. On my way out I smiled at that fucker and told him: 'Better luck next time and if someone tells you to fuck off, just fuck off".

CHAPTER TEN

IT'S GONNA BE ALRIGHT

My brother and his friend came to pick me up and we went to Italy together. Meanwhile, all the guys with whom I trained in Börgönd were transported to Szeged, given civilian clothes and given orders to track me down.

My brother and his friend had to cross the border illegally just to come and get me. So they took a big risk. I had to sleep on the street in Yugoslavia for three days until my brother and his friend came to pick me up, because I had no money. So I slept on benches and in the bushes. I found a construction site so I could climb the fence and sleep on the flat roof.

I slept at Belgrade train station, at the very back where they keep the empty trains. It was OK for a while and then the police arrived. I could barely understand them. They checked my passport and told me I was a long way from where I should be. I only had the 'small' passport and I was in Belgrade, way beyond its remit.

They were two big motherfuckers and I was shitting in my pants when they took my passport, but still I thought I have to run before I get locked up. But as I was planning my escape, they returned my passport and told me to go away so that I wouldn't be their problem anymore. So after that, I hid in bushes during the day so I wouldn't be noticed.

We had arranged that after two days I would go to the

train station every second hour and they would be on one of those trains. They arrived. It was amazing to see my brother again, but we couldn't hang around. We had to move fast.

He said it would be easy to cross the border, we simply had to buy a ticket from Belgrade to Sežana and then get off the train just before the Italian border and cross over to Villa Opicina. There were guards on the train checking passports before the border, but I was so tired by then that no matter how hard I tried to stay up I fell asleep so I didn't notice anything.

My brother woke me up when we arrived and said there was a guard coming, but luckily he just stuck his head in, saw there were six of us in one booth and he just went away. We didn't look suspicious. We jumped off before the border, at Sežana, the last station and snuck out of Yugoslavia by the same route that my brother and his friend had come into the country, it was just empty agricultural land.

Then we went to Villa Opicina, the first station in Italy, and caught the next train, destination Venice. When they were coming to meet me, my brother and his friend had befriended a guy who drew people's portraits, in St Mark's Plaza in Venice and they had slept one night at his place. He was a gay guy, who had taken a shine to the Polish friend of my brother, so we looked him up and he agreed that we could stay with him again.

So we slept at his place and that was the first time that I smoked hash. I didn't know what it looked like because it was already rolled up. The next morning, our host left early for work, while we were still there, so we took the opportunity to search for his hash. My brother explained that it looked like chocolate, probably in tin foil. I found a big lump, but in light of our host generous hospitality, we only cut a small piece off. He probably would have given it to us if we had asked, but he wasn't there, so what choice did we have?

It was the beginning of October but warm and I felt so happy compared to a week ago when I was in the military hating my life. And now I was in Venice and the sun was shining, I felt very lucky and happy to be there. I hadn't been in any western countries before. I'd been in Yugoslavia which was nice and Romania and Bulgaria, but they were shittier than Hungary. So that wasn't a step forward, it was a step back.

We've been back to Venice since then and it is much worse now – so overcrowded. Everyone can afford to travel; tourism is so cheap. When I first sat by the Trevi Fountain in Rome, there was hardly anyone there. But the last time I went there with you Viki, we had to fight through the crowd just to throw some change into the fountain. The whole square was crowded, not just the fountain. Back in the eighties, everywhere I went, there were very few people and everyone was friendly.

So I was feeling very lucky in Venice even though I had no money, no job, no passport. I was young and didn't really care. We went sightseeing a little bit and then we headed to Bologna where we spent the night. We wanted to sleep in an abandoned house in the suburbs but it was already occupied. We were scared and ran away. Eventually we slept under a bridge.

The next morning, a Sunday, we set off for Perugia and slept there as well and then the day after that we arrived in Latina, a beach resort an hour from Rome, the capital of the province of Latina in the Lazio region, in central Italy, and one of the cities where refugees could stay and where my brother had been living. I remained there until Christmas.

My brother had been there for a year and he spoke Italian so perfectly, people thought he was a native. He is very good at languages, he can pick up any language very quickly. Latina had a refugee camp at that time, but there were so many of us that they had to rent small hotels out and put refugees in those hotels. My brother was in a hotel on the seaside. Literally, across the road from the hotel was the beach. The hotel called Hotel Caty and it was on Via Lungomare in Latina.

The people in Italy were very friendly. I haven't seen anything like that before. In Hungary when I had to work I was always rushed. In Italy when I worked in the market or when I was delivering pianos even as a political refugee, people were always friendly and said 'piano piano' which means gradually, take it easy, don't rush. I remember one time my flip-flop broke when I was working on the market and when an older woman who was selling flip-flops saw it, she just gave me one for free and I wasn't even working for her.

Another time, when we were delivering a piano with my brother and an older Hungarian guy who ran the business and lived in Italy, we got to the delivery address just before 'siesta', took the piano up to the second floor and wanted to leave. The father of the family insisted that he wouldn't pay unless we sat down with the family and had lunch with them. So we had no choice but to sit down with the family and enjoy lunch. It was like being in a restaurant. There was no rush to eat our food and the mother served us just as if we were her own family. We had a few glasses of wine as well and talked a lot about Hungary and life as a political refugee in Italy. The lunch and the talking lasted for about an hour and when we left the father not only paid us but gave us tips and a bottle of wine.

My brother was in Italy because he had been kicked out of Austria, so we only stayed in Italy for a few months before our next trip. We had many friends in Austria, so we decided to spend the holidays, Christmas and New Year with them, but we had no passport. My brother said it would be just as easy to get into Austria as it had been to cross the Italy-Yugoslavia border.

CHAPTER ELEVEN

ALL THE WAY

I think it was Christmas Day when we left Latina and went to Austria. Unfortunately, we only arrived in Vienna after Christmas, as our first attempt had failed. They caught us on the train and sent us back to Latina. From there we tried to find someone who might be able to take us by car to the border so that we would be less suspicious. Then our Hungarian friend Reaper (nick-named not after the Grim Reaper, but because he cut the grass in the Latina camp with a scythe) said that he knew someone who would take us and that he would come with us, if we didn't mind. Reaper was one of our best friends in Latina, so we were glad he wanted to come too. That is how we became the three Hungarian refugees: my brother, Reaper and me.

It was winter and the border was hard to cross because of the snow. We did the same thing as before – got off the train in Italy close to the border and then crossed over on foot – but it took us hours in the thick snow and we were frozen. We reached the station in Austria very early in the morning, much too early – that made us stand out like wet frozen Hungarian refugees in a respectable Austrian railway station. But we desperately needed to warm up by sitting on the radiators and hanging our clothes on them to dry. The best time to turn up would have been when the station was busier. There were no trains running this early.

Big mistake.

Inevitably someone called the police, because those boys in blue suddenly appeared and escorted us to the police station. It was a three-way border – Italy, Austria and Yugoslavia – so we told the police that we had come from Hungary through Yugoslavia. They didn't know any different.

The refugee camp was in Traiskirchen in Austria, so we told them we were refugees from Hungary and so they gave us a free tickets to Traiskirchen. We were supposed to change trains at Vienna and then travel on to the refugee camp 30km to the south, but we stopped at Vienna to visit our friends, and stayed there. We all gave false names because we planned to go back to Italy in a week and because if we ever wanted to return in the future, we could. I was Zoltán Kovács at that time.

Among my friends in Vienna was Güzü, whom I was very happy to meet, because we had not seen each other for a long time. Our first serious party was, of course, New Year's Eve. Since the guys had lived in Vienna for some time by then, they had contacts with the locals so we could easily get drugs. They obtained weed (marijuana) and trip (LSD). I hadn't had any luck with trip before, but I was very happy to give it a try. However, mixing the weed and trip with lots of alcohol brought the desired effect. I hadn't laughed that much in my life before. I completely lost my sense of time. I remember that when we set off for a punk party from our friend's place, who probably lived on the third floor, it seemed as if we had gone down from the 100th floor, the flight of stairs was never ending. Of course, I laughed at that too.

When we finally got down, we found other things to laugh at. For example, if I asked someone in Italy what time it was, they told me the time and even invited me for a cup of coffee. Here in Vienna, people just turned away and rushed away from us. We got to the punk party pretty slowly. My friends already knew some Viennese punks, so we got in easily. As I mentioned kids, we partied a lot in Hungary too and there were some interesting looking guys there as well, but this was something else. First, it was in Vienna and we were unfamiliar with everybody and secondly, it was full of very colourful characters. It was an experience to meet them. Sometime the next morning we staggered back to our friend's place.

The life here was certainly better than in Italy. The weather wasn't as nice and there was no seaside, but we had plenty of money and Vienna is a nice city. In Italy we got given food and accommodation and we could do odd jobs, but we were basically broke. We could help market people set up their stalls or deliver pianos for very poor money and we had to work very hard for it.

In Austria, I made good money from shoplifting. It was very easy to shoplift in Vienna at that time. Nobody was watching anybody. Austrian people, they trusted each other not to steal and they made enough money to buy their stuff, but we were from Hungary, we had nothing. We'd walked into a simple supermarket and were ecstatic because it all seemed so luxurious.

My brother and Reaper only stayed for a week or so and went back to Italy. My brother asked me to go back with them, but I was adamant because the Viennese lifestyle was much closer to the life I left and adored in Hungary, than the life in Italy. That's why after my brother went back to Italy, I registered in Traiskirchen camp as a political refugee as Zoltán Kovács. I didn't want to use my real name because I promised my brother that I would go back to Italy in a few months.

When I registered as political refugee, my friends accompanied me and I remember when my name was called – 'Zoltán Kovács please come in' – I didn't respond. I think it was Güzü who poked me and said, 'Hey Zotya, that was for you, go!'

I was assigned a bunk bed and given a blanket and a pillow, a tin plate, a tin cup and cutlery. The next morning after an early, army style, alarm call, I was given a breakfast of coffee or tea and crusty bread rolls with butter and jam which were dispensed in the dormitory by camp workers out of large metal jugs and wooden crates.

I was quarantined in this dormitory until 19th January, 1987, until they had checked whether or not I was an internationally wanted criminal, and if I could stay in Austria as a political refugee. Since I was just starting my 'career', they didn't find anything wrong with me. Out of my friends from Szeged, Güzü was in Austria, which I already mentioned, but there was also Szkuri and Doxen, as well as Gyuszika. After the New Year's Eve party, Güzü returned to his hotel in Göttshach, where he officially lived.

There were many nationalities in the camp, but during my time there, mostly Hungarians, Poles, Bulgarians, Romanians and Albanians. Gangs of Albanians would beat people up for money. Some people were murdered. The Albanians were Muslims, while the rest of us were Christians, so for us they were the strangest and for some reason the dirtiest and most miserable and violent too. They always left the common areas (shower, toilet) very dirty. Instead of toilet paper, they used water bottles, which wasn't a problem in itself, but I didn't like their habit of tossing them around everywhere.

The Albanians always caused trouble, fortunately, mostly to each other, but to other people as well. They stabbed, robbed and broke into other people's rooms and ransacked them. Therefore, the rooms had to be cons-tantly locked. That's why we usually spent the nights with someone who was accommodated in a hotel or we rented a hotel in Vienna when we 'worked' there.

The camp building itself actually looked nothing like a prison; it was more like a large military academy four storeys high, with a gleaming white front elevation, and three serried ranks of about fifty windows set atop a row of arched windows. The building was surrounded by acres of manicured lawn and beyond that, in the distance, acres of vineyards – this was an important wine growing region.

From the outside, everything looked orderly, clean, regal, even palatial, but what happened inside those immaculate white walls was in stark contrast to its outward appearance. I remember thinking at the time how very Austrian that was – hiding so much unpleasantness from public view behind such a pristine facade. Also, the camp's German name, 'Flüchtlingslager' which literally translates to 'refugee storage' was so faultlessly clinical and dehumanizing that it was almost comical.

Indeed, the camp was initially built in 1900 as the Artillery Cadet School. During World War II it was upgraded into an elite training centre for the education and indoctrination of the most promising hand-selected members of the Hitler Youth in the region, to prepare them for future Nazi Party leadership.

But by the time I arrived in the late eighties, we were already beginning to wear out our welcome (not least because people like me and my friends lived up to our stereotype as professional thieves).

If I close my eyes now, I can still picture the long corridors, its floors tiled with a repeating red and beige diamond pattern, its huge dormitories with oak parquet floors and row upon row of metal bunk beds.

My original accommodation was in the camp in Traiskirchen, but as soon as I got out of quarantine, Szkuri, Doxen and Gyuszika were already waiting for me, so luckily I didn't have to sleep there. I say 'luckily' because the camp was worse than a prison. It was a violent, overcrowded hellhole, so I didn't want to stay there, even though I had been assigned a private room after my quarantine ended – it transpired that the huge noisy dormitories were temporary holding areas. After the quarantine, I was free to come and go as I pleased and so I continued my 'career' in Austria with Szkuri, Doxen and Gyuszika, which meant we went together to steal in and around Vienna.

When we were caught by the police in Austria, I had told them a fake name, Zoltán Kovács, because I thought I was going back to Italy, so I could tell them whatever I want. So I was registered in Traiskirchen under a fake name, but as soon as I decided to stay in Austria, I confessed that it wasn't my real name and that I wanted to register under my real name. They said that was fine but that it would take some time to process, so in the meantime because I had no papers, I should stay in the camp in Traiskirchen.

I had such a good time that even though I had promised my brother that I would go to Italy in a few months, I still stayed in Austria. I told them that at the border, when they caught me and when I registered here in Traiskirchen as a political refugee, I said that I was Zoltán Kovács because I had escaped from the military in Hungary and I didn't know whether Austria would extradite me to face charges back home or not. I had been sentenced to ten years in prison in Hungary, so there was no question, I could not go back there, no matter what. However, I told them that once I was convinced that this danger was not a threat, I would like to live in my own name in the future. There was nothing wrong with this, they fully understood and started arranging my name change. The only problem with this was that I could not leave Traiskirchen until I received the ID card in my own name, as the one in the name of Zoltán Kovács had been taken away, so I was left without an ID card. Of course, I didn't wait for it and continued to roam around Austria with my friends.

We stole a lots of alcohol and food from stores called

Billa, because it had a huge variety of everything compare to Hungary and sold things we had never seen before and of course it was very easy to steal from it. Johnnie Walker, Ballantine, Chivas Regal and similar drinks we could sell at half price to a Hungarian guy, who ran a 'canteen' at the refugee camp in Traiskirchen and sold them by shots to the people living there (mostly to Hungarians). In addition to alcohol, we also stole clothes, Walkmans, cameras and similar small electronic items if someone ordered them.

I don't remember exactly when my friends bought our first car – a Lada –from some Hungarian guy, while I was in quarantine or a little bit later but I do remember that we travelled everywhere in that Lada.

I had the final adventure with our little Lada after we broke down on the motorway one night. I was with Szkuri and Doxen. Only they had driving licences, so they always drove. After we broke down they left for help and I stayed in the car. It was already morning and they were nowhere to be seen. Suddenly, a large Mercedes with a German license plate pulled up in front of me. It turned out that the driver was a Hungarian living in Germany who had seen the Hungarian license plate on the Lada and wanted to help. He offered to tow me to a nearby service centre where there was a petrol station and a restaurant. Since my friends hadn't returned and I was afraid of what would happen if next time a police officer stops by the car and I have no ID card so I accepted his offer. I didn't have a driving licence back then and I've never driven in my life, but I thought it would be just a tow, and nothing bad would happen. I soon found out how wrong I was.

He connected the two cars with the tow rope and we sat in the two driver's seats. We set off pretty slowly in the outside lane. I started my windshield wipers as it was rainy. The muddy water from the motorway hit me so hard I could barely see. Everything went well until the battery died. Within a short time I couldn't see anything, so I pulled down the window and waved to the guy to stop. Luckily, he noticed me and pulled over. I told him what the problem was and quickly cleaned the windshield. He asked me to leave the window down and look out of it while steering as he was in a hurry and didn't have time to stop every mile to clean my windshield. I told him no problem, I would stick my head out the window and drive like that for the rest of the way.

We sat back in the cars. Then I had the idea that since the battery was already dead, I would turn off the ignition. So I did it and we set off again pretty slowly. We went very well until for some reason I had to turn the steering wheel to the left and it locked. From there, my car pretty slowly started to drift into the inner lanes. I pushed the brakes with full force, but our little Lada was no match for the big Mercedes. I waved out of the window again to stop, but now the guy either didn't notice or was no longer interested because he was in a big hurry.

As I weaved around the lanes, so did he, until I made contact with the metal cordon on the inside lane. He didn't even stop after that, but I think after a while he must have woken up and noticed the tsunami of sparks that was arching from the side of my car as I scraped along the metal cordon. Or maybe it was the deafening scraping noise that alerted him. Finally he stopped. I could see that he was starting to lose his patience, but he held it together, although by now his act of kindness had most definitely turned sour. We both wanted this journey to end as quickly and painlessly as possible.

After I took the steering lock off the car, we set off for a third time. Since we were in the inner lane, we had to drive pretty slowly into the outside lane. The traffic was already quite bad by then, so it wasn't easy. It involved a lots of acceleration and deceleration. At the time, I didn't know the main rule of towing was that the tow rope should always remain tight, because if it loosens and the towing car accelerates, the sudden tension could snap the tow rope. That's exactly what had happened. I was kind of lucky because the car still had enough momentum so that I could pull over and stop on the hard shoulder.

The guy also stopped and jumped out of his car. This time he couldn't keep calm. In fact, he completely lost it. He jumped up, buried his head in both hands and yelled: 'I don't believe it. How did you ever pass your test? You're the worst driver I've ever met in my life. Did you bribe the driving instructor? How much did you pay him? You shouldn't be on the road. I can't understand how anyone could think you have the first idea about handling a car. I mean, Jesus. You're clueless. I've never seen anything like it'.

I waited until he had vented his anger and worn himself out a little, then I said quietly, 'I don't have a driving licence. My friends just left me to guard the car, not to drive it'. I will never forget the look on his face and the way he stared at me. Without a word, he sat back in his car, backed up, got out, tied together the torn tow rope, sat back in his car and just said 'Let's go'. I sat back in our little Lada and we embarked on the seemingly endless journey again. Within 10–15 minutes, we had arrived at the rest area. We stopped nicely, the guy got out of his car, took off his tow rope, tossed it in his trunk and stormed away so quickly I could hardly thank him.

I sat down in the restaurant to eat, hoping that my friends would find me there. They arrived within a few hours. A Hungarian guy brought them in his car. They laughed hard when I told them about my little adventure, but they quickly stopped when they saw our Lada. It was no longer worth spending money on, so we sold it for parts to another Hungarian guy and we bought a blue Opel Kadett because we needed a reliable car. Since gaining my licence, I have learned that it's harder to be towed than to drive.

We made very good money from shoplifting , twice as much as people working. On the Mariahilfer Straße there were lots of Hungarian owned stores. Hungarians would come on day trips to buy electrical goods there. If you could get out of Hungary, that was the place to buy the stuff we didn't have in Hungary. So Hungarian refugees were employed to entice fellow Hungarians into the shops. It was hard work, standing for hours and trying to persuade people to visit the employer's shop, whilst remaining upbeat and enthusiastic. It was very competitive, because there were lots of people in the street doing the same thing.

They'd tell the Hungarians that it was great quality, but it was the shittiest quality in Austria, so it was a kind of rip off, but they would buy it anyway. They couldn't go into any other store because they were too expensive and you had to speak German. These shopping tourists hardly saw the town; they were dropped off by bus in the morning and spent the day shopping and would be collected again in the evening.

I couldn't entice fellow Hungarians into the shops at all. Shoplifting suited me better. My friends were very good at it. First they shoplifted some nice clothes for me because you have to look nice to go into the shop and make the shopkeeper think that you have enough money to buy something. So you have to steal some clothes to make it easier to steal clothes. When you walk in somewhere wearing the same brand, you look like a customer, so the shopkeeper thinks: 'Ah ok, these guys shop around here'.

Our outfits were always good quality and smart casual so we wouldn't appear suspicious. My favourite brands were Fred Perry, Lewis, Diesel, Hugo Boss, Lonsdale, Dr Marten and the American Bomber Jacket. We weren't too elegant – no suits and ties – because I think that would have been suspicious too, but our outfits looked very good. I haven't had a wardrobe like that since because I can't afford to buy it from my earnings.

In June 2014, I flew back from England and Tigi flew from Australia to Vienna so we could celebrate our birthdays together and visit all the places we had been in our youth.

Tigi & me in Vienna on our birthday in the Prater

In my era, Mariahilfer Straße was a bustling street full of people and traffic. Following a national political debate, it has recently been transformed into a paved pedestrian shopping boulevard with outdoor furniture including benches, water elements and planters with flowering trees. I'm not sure whether that would have made any harder or easier for me and my friends to ply our dishonest trade but who cares? The major obstacle to shoplifting today is without doubt with alarms at every shop's door and the ubiquitous surveillance cameras inside and outside the shops. I certainly wouldn't like to try my chances there today.

In the eighties, the employees in front of the shops had the task of luring the customers inside to buy some goods. We called these guys 'felhajtók' and we had a good mutual relationship. We made lots of money for each other. If they needed alcohol, clothes, a CD or a good quality CD player, camera, camcorder or almost anything we could steal, they ordered it from us and we brought it to them at half price within a few days. However, we were able to steal much more than the 'felhajtók' ordered. Then we would leave our haul with them and if they could sell items for more than half the price, it was their profit. This was good for everybody. The Hungarian buyer received good quality goods, cheaper than the crap he would have bought in the store; the 'felhajtók' also earned some money and we got half the retail price. This was really a win-win situation. Of course, we were also able to sell a lots of stolen goods in Traiskirchen. As I mentioned earlier, our best man for this was the Hungarian guy who ran the 'canteen'.

Our 'normal' days consisted of waking up between 10:00–12:00am – just like you kids on the weekend – and tidying ourselves up (dry heaving, showering, brushing teeth, breakfast). Before we left, of course we had a couple of beers and whiskeys.

After we finished our morning drink (I don't mean coffee or tea), we set off to 'work'. If there were some orders, we tried to fulfill those first because it was guaranteed money, right away. If there was no order, then we just went from store to store and stole things that were easy to steal and sell. Over time, we got to know the shops and where to go, but we always found new ones too. Of course, we didn't go into the same store twice in a row because it would have been suspicious. We had to visit shops over a wide area so that we didn't raise suspicion. Since we usually went to the shops in pairs to steal, the other pair could go in because there were usually four of us, but it was not recommended for the same pair. In a pair, one of us would watch the sellers or just distract them whilst the other one stole the goods.

In bigger stores with more shop assistants we'd go in a group. Let's say, two guys would keep the shopkeeper busy in a corner, asking for help, where he or she couldn't see the rest of us. Because we went into the shop many times, the other two knew where the good stuff was, so they didn't waste any time and they'd take as much as they could.

'Panyóka' style in my favourite Lonsdale T-shirt & bomber jacket in Germany

We usually hid the stolen goods under our shirts, which were tucked into our pants. We always put a T-shirt under the shirt so that the stolen goods wouldn't stick to our skin and we could slide them back easily and quickly. Our jackets – we always wore baggy jackets, no matter what the brand – covered goods bulging out from under our shirt. When it was warm, we put our jackets on our shoulders and packed the stolen goods on only one side, or just put them under our armpits. With this technique, we could steal larger things, such as a VCR. The shoulder jacket method was called 'panyóka' after the uniform of Hungarian Hussars.

Of course, after a successful 'action' we always had to drink something, so by the time our 'work' ended, we were in a very good mood. With the 'loot' we found our buyers and picked up our 'salary'. It was usually between 4–5pm and by that time we were hungry as well, so we would find a restaurant and as the expression goes: 'We ate, drank and didn't grieve'. After the restaurant we either went to a pub to continue drinking or bought some beer, stole a few bottles of spirits and if there was no drugs left from the day before, we bought some of those too. Then we went to our 'main accommodation' and continued partying there until everyone passed out. The next day we started all over again.

As I mentioned earlier, kids, after our little Lada broke down and was damaged beyond repair during towing, we bought a blue Opel Kadett and continued our 'career' with it. What I didn't mention was that, just like the Lada, I gave our Opel the 'coup de grâce' too.

We were at Gyuszika's hotel somewhere near Linz when I decided that I wanted to learn how to drive a car. Of course, I was drinking but I wasn't drunk. Szkuri and Doxen, the two drivers didn't mind teaching me but Gyuszika was against it because he had heard the story about my 'joyride' in the Lada. That pissed me off because we had bought the Opel together. As I got drunker and drunker, I got angrier and angrier so I decided to piss them off. For some reason we had yellow spray paint in the trunk so I painted a swastika on the hood of the trunk and then went back to the hotel to continue drinking with them.

We wanted to go to Traiskirchen later to sell some goods, so Doxen wasn't drinking. It was his turn to be the designated driver. So when we came to leave they saw my 'paint job'. Well kids, they were not happy. They had to paint the whole hood yellow before we could leave.

When we arrived at Traiskirchen, Doxen and Gyuszika

went into the camp to sell the goods whilst Szkuri and I waited in the car. I got bored so I asked Szkuri if I could drive. He wasn't too drunk, but drunk enough to say 'yes'. So I started driving and it went well. I had no problem with changing the gears or steering the car. As you know, my father was a driving instructor for years so when I was a kid I spent lots of time in the car when he was teaching people how to drive. I felt certain that I'd be able to drive a car at the first opportunity.

I was cruising around nicely until we reached a junction with a stop sign almost totally obscured by vegetation, plus it was getting dark, so I missed it. Unfortunately, another car was coming and it was too late for me to stop. I hit the back of the other car. The damage wasn't too bad and no one was injured, but my friend Szkuri panicked, jumped out of the car and ran 'into the woods'. The driver of the other car got out too, but seeing Szkuri running away, he froze and just watched what was happening.

I chased after Szkuri into a small copse of trees, then I stood still and listened. I knew he must have stopped running because I would have heard his footsteps. That meant he was hiding.

'Szkuri,' I yelled. 'Szkuri. We need to go back to the car. Come on. You're only making it worse. Szkuriiiiiii'.

Silence. I tried again.

'Look, I know you can hear me. The police are going be here soon and they'll know it's us because we're the registered owners. The best thing we can do is to deal with this now. We can't run away... Szkuri, please'.

A few moments later, Szkuri suddenly stepped out from behind a tree. He was three feet away from me. In the half-light, I nearly shat myself.

'Aiiaaargggh! Jesus, you scared the shit out of me. I thought you were a bear. Oh God'. After gathering my composure, I added, 'So… are you coming, or what?'

Without saying a word, Szkuri started jogging slowly in the direction of the car. Thinking my calm head and my rational little pep talk had brought him to his senses, I started plodding back towards the car, with a huge feeling of relief. I also felt a little bit proud of my powers of persuasion.

When I was twenty yards away from the car, I realised I couldn't have been more wrong. Szkuri was simply rescuing his bag. He grabbed it from the back seat and then legged it again, in the opposite direction. So I had to sprint after him again. As I passed the driver of the other car, I shouted, 'It's OK, I'm coming back'. The driver watched incredulously as he witnessed the most inefficient and indecisive hit and run in the history of motoring.

Somehow I managed to catch up with Szkuri, whereupon I launched myself at his feet and rugby tackled him to the ground. We landed in a damp patch of earth. I was covered with mud but somehow Szkuri didn't have a mark on him, which of course, he found hilarious. He couldn't stop laughing. But at least he'd stopped running.

'Look, mate,' I said, trying to catch my breath. 'The shit is going to hit the fan… much more if we run away. We're the… registered owners, so they're going to catch us anyway. So please… come back. You've got a clean licence… and shirt and trousers. We can say that you were driving. OK?'

'Yeah, OK,' replied Szkuri, sulkily.

'Great. Come on, let's go and talk to the man'.

'I wasn't running away,' said Szkuri, 'I just needed a piss'.

'And I didn't just scream like a girl back by the trees. By the way, the other two don't need to know about this'.

A few moments later, the police arrived and Szkuri told them he was driving, showed them his driving licence and the insurance policy and by some miracle they believed him. They didn't even breathalyse either of us. Everything was fine, except our Opel, which was completely buggered.

After the police left, we pushed the car to the side of the road and trudged back to the camp in the dark. Of course, Doxen and Gyuszika had already been waiting for us for hours. When they heard our story, they started yelling and cursing but after about 10 minutes they ran out of words and oxygen so we decided to spend the night in the camp.

Like I said, my original accommodation was in Traiskirchen so I had a room and a bed to sleep in. After everybody found a place to sleep we met up in the canteen. Because we supplied the booze, we didn't have to pay for it, we just had to replace it the next day.

After I don't know how many drinks, I blurted out to Szkuri: 'Shit, I feel really bad now. We fucked the car. It's our fault'.

'You mean it's your fault,' replied Szkuri, 'You're the one who can't drive and you crashed the car'.

'Technically, it was the council's fault, because someone should have cut the hedge. I couldn't see the stop sign. I couldn't see it. Not my fault. No one could have seen that. Not even Alain Prost, it was almost completely hidden. I mean, did you see it?'

'I dunno,' replied Szkuri. 'I wasn't driving. I wasn't watching the road'.

'But mate, I can't drive. You should have been looking out for me'.

'Can I be honest with you?' asked Szkuri.

'What a stupid question! You can only be honest with me, you're my friend. I don't want to hear a lie from you, I have my enemies for that'.

'Well, if you hadn't painted that Nazi shit on the car in the first place, that other guy wouldn't have even been at the junction and so we wouldn't have hit him at all'.

'What? Ah shit, now you're getting metaphysical. You're doing my head in. That's like time travel or something. Fuck, I'm so pissed'.

'So what do you want to do?'

'There's only one thing for it, Szkuri, 'barátom'. We're gonna… we're gonna have to have to steal a car. To make it good, make it up to—'

'That's a fucking great idea. Let's do that then. But first, I have to puke'.

So we staggered out of the canteen and after Szkuri had attended to his nausea, we went off to steal a car.

There were lots of Eastern European cars parked around the camp because many refugees brought their cars with them. So we found a Lada because Szkuri told me that he could steal it. He was only half right. He was able to start it but after the first turn the steering wheel locked so we had to abandon the car at the side of the road.

After our little adventure we returned to the canteen and continued drinking with the others. We drank and drank and I don't know what happened later. All I know is that I woke up in my room in my bed in the morning. I had a very bad hangover and it took me several minutes to realise where I was. I had all my clothes on and my money in my pocket so I was OK to find my friends.

My roommates were sitting at the table watching me getting up and preparing to leave. I had the top bunk. When I looked down I saw a huge puddle on the floor.

'What the fuck?' I said. 'Who did this? I could break my neck, slipping on that. Guys, if you're going to get all house proud and wash the floor, at least do a proper job, so I don't have to wade through your shit'.

There was a brief stony silence. 'You mean, wade through your own piss,' said one of the guys, through gritted teeth.

'Yeah,' added the other one, pointing and waggling his finger accusingly at the puddle.

'What do you mean?' I asked, trying to maintain the moral high ground but I was already developing the sickening notion that I'd done something wrong again.

They exchanged an angry glance and then with faux exaggerated patience the bravest explained: 'Last night you fell asleep early. You were out of it. Totally shit-faced. We stayed up playing cards, but after a while you woke up again and needed to take a leak, but the door was locked, so you pissed all over the fucking floor. So, that puddle isn't our shit; it is quite literally – your piss'.

My temples were throbbing. I surveyed my watery domain and decided to brazen it out. 'Well either way it's your fault,' I retorted dismissively, 'because you didn't give me a key and that's why I couldn't go out to use the toilet so you should clean it up. I'd love to stay longer, but I have to be somewhere'.

Scraping the barrel to summon every last vestige of my dignity, I hopped jauntily from the top bunk, careened stiffly out of the room, vomited copiously in the corridor and then slunk silently away to find a ditch to die in.

Because we didn't have a car we had to hire Hungarians with cars to drive us when we were 'working' outside Vienna. We paid for petrol and we either gave them money for the day or we stole something they wanted. That was how we got dropped off again one day at Gyuszika's hotel, near Linz.

Gyuszika lived in a small village which was nice and quiet whenever we weren't there getting drunk. As usual, we were partying noisily, so someone called the police on us. I wasn't supposed to leave the refugee camp because I didn't have my new ID card with my own name on it so things ended badly again. I was thrown in jail, under my own name even if I told the truth. They tried to phone the refugee camp to check my story, but it was the weekend so they received no answer and chucked me in jail. If I had simply pretended to be Zoltán Kovács, they wouldn't have been able to do anything. If they had just waited until Monday, they could have phoned the camp to verify my story, but they just decided that I was lying and they transferred me from that small village to Linz, which was the closest big city. I spent two months in a big city jail.

Another problem was, at that time I was a skinhead. I liked the music and the clothes, but I didn't really hate anyone and I wasn't violent. I had my Dr Marten boots on, a Levis jeans with a Lonsdale T-shirt and my bomber jacket. Anyway, we had this bad habit that when someone got drunk and passed out, we'd prank them. We might steal their ID papers and write in it that he was in a mental institution or draw a swastika on their forehead and hide the mirrors.

When the police arrested me I had to undress. They hated me – 'rough' looking Hungarian skinhead. But that all changed when I took my socks off and saw that my nails had been painted red. They couldn't stop laughing at me. I'd been pranked while I was passed out drunk. I prayed they didn't assume I was gay and put me in a cell with a violent prisoner who would see me as an easy target and try to take advantage of me.

Actually, the jail was OK; it wasn't a violent place. It was much better than the camp in Traiskirchen. I was trapped, but at least I didn't fear for my life. As I mentioned kids, back in Hungary I had skinhead and punk friends and they were friends with each other, but these two groups hated each other in the West. As I mentioned kids just now, I wasn't a violent skinhead, I liked the music and the clothes. But it didn't help my treatment whenever I got arrested by the police.

After two months, I spoke to a lawyer. I wasn't sentenced, I was told that I could go but I had just a week to leave Austria. I had paperwork which said that if I didn't leave within a week I could be rearrested and then I'd be sent back to prison. They kept me in jail just to teach me a lesson, because they could have checked who I was within a few days and let me go, maybe they did check and that is why I wasn't sentenced.

As you see kids, I was in Austria for five months but I spent two of them in jail. Huge career.

CHAPTER TWELVE

I CAN'T MAKE IT ON TIME

I made my way back to the refugee camp and found I still had a room there where I could sleep. Of course, it wasn't my own room because I just couldn't show my face there after the 'accident' the last time I slept there. I spent the night and the next morning I tried to find my friends. I stole some booze and sold it to my canteen friend, so I could get some money. I knew I had to find one of my friends soon, before I got caught again. I tracked down my good friend Güzü who was still living in Göttshach. I stayed with him and his wife in my last days in Austria. It took me about ten days to find someone who could take me to the border, so when a friend with a car eventually drove me to the Italian border, I was already over my time limit.

It was May, so there was no problem with snow this time. Nice and easy. I crossed the border and took a train to Ferrara where I went to the police station and told them that I came from Hungary through Yugoslavia and I wanted to go to Latina and register as a political refugee. But this time, I couldn't give them my real name because I was already registered under that name in Italy so I called myself Zoltán Boldog (Happy). The name suited me because I was always happy and smiling.

I wanted to meet up with my brother, but this time I couldn't just say I wanted to share a hotel with him, because I was using a fake name. But I did at least manage to register to Canada as the country I wanted to settle in. My brother had also registered there, because the admin could take up to two years until they accepted someone, and he wanted to stay in Italy as long as possible.

After a month, they transferred me from Latina to Rome, where I lived for four months in two different refugee hotels. I only remember the last one's name because the first was just temporary and for only a week or so. So I spent most of my time in Hotel Claudia on Via Bartolomeo Eustachio, just 20 minutes' walk from Termini and a little over 30 minutes' walk from Trevi Fountain and our favourite hangout, the Spanish Steps where we bought our drugs. I could come and go as I wanted. If I didn't sleep there, it didn't raise any alarms. I couldn't work legally, had no money, but a place to sleep and all my meals.

We travelled light. We just had a backpack, full of whatever we needed the most, although my Dr Martens boots – bought with some money from my parents – and my bomber jacket were my constant companions, plus sunglasses. I also had a favourite burgundy Lonsdale T-shirt, with yellow writing, that Tigi had stolen for me. I wore that a lot as you kids can see it on the picture earlier in the book.

I stayed in Rome from June until October and I enjoyed a very good summer and early autumn there with my friends. It was there I met a guy called Csaszi, a refugee who had registered in Germany. We went everywhere together. Then we could go to any of the famous tourist attractions, like the Trevi Fountain or the Spanish Steps to enjoy a cold beer and nobody was pushing us around, we didn't have to jostle for position because the crowd was always small. We just enjoyed the weather and hanging out, talking.

One day, a guy from our hotel asked us to buy some

weed because he had never tried it before. He said if we bought it, we could all smoke it together. We agreed, so we all went to the Spanish Steps and bought some weed. We smoked a joint and then bought some beer in a nearby shop and sat by the Trevi Fountain to drink them. We were having fun, talking and laughing, even the new guy.

Among us there was an older guy who wanted to get the most out of the freebie, so he suggested we roll another joint. We told him we'd wait a little bit longer because of the new guy. But he kept pushing the new guy, until he agreed to roll another one. By the time we had smoked the second joint, it was dark, so we went to a nearby pub where the booze was cheap.

The new guy paid for the beers and we went outside to drink them because the weather was nice. We were having so much fun, that we hadn't noticed that the new guy had disappeared. Next thing we knew, a crowd had gathered outside the pub and we heard yelling. Then we noticed that the new guy was missing, so we rushed over to the crowd where the new guy was lying on the pavement, crying in pain. The idiot older guy was trying to grab his hand and help him up: 'Come mate, let's get out of here before someone calls the police'. We told him to fuck off.

The new guy looked in a bad way. We could tell that his leg was broken and probably his arm too. After the older guy ran away, the rest of us waited for the ambulance and made sure that the new guy was properly taken care of. When we visited him later in the hospital, we learned that one of his legs and both his arms were broken.

Csaszi wanted to rob the poor guy in his hospital bed. He reasoned: 'What can he do? He can't get up and he can't use any of his arms'. 'Fuck you,' I replied, 'that's fucking low! You can't come to the hospital if you want to rob him'. So he changed his mind but I should have known then that he couldn't be trusted. He just looked out for himself and no one else. Unfortunately, I only learned that later when he screwed me over in Hungary after I tried to help him.

In the hospital, we asked the new guy what had happened. He told us that he felt like climbing up a building but when he got so high and looked down, he got scared and froze. And then, he had reasoned that it was probably just a dream so he should wake himself up by letting go. He woke up alright. I went to Spain before he got out of the hospital so I don't know for sure, but I suspect that was his first and last experiment with weed.

When we were in Spain, we heard that another good friend of ours had been sitting on the railings of a balcony, lost his balance and fell several storeys to his death. He'd been smoking weed too. So kids, what can we learn from this? When you're stoned, you have to be extra careful. Fortunately, for his friends who were with him, before he died, the poor guy was able to tell the police that no one had pushed him.

We did a bit of shoplifting in Rome, a few clothes so we could sell them for drugs, and we also stole lots of booze. But it was harder to steal in Rome than in Austria. We stole only what we need to live from day to day, not to make lots of spare cash. I remember one time, after my brother left for Canada, I went back to the camp in Latina to visit friends with lots of bottles of stolen wine. I sold many of them but we also drank lots too. Of course, I passed out and the next morning when I gained consciousness on the lower bunk of the bed, I yelled 'Oh no, I'm in jail again!' Luckily, this wasn't the case, but the beds in the camp in Latina were very similar to the ones in jail. Everybody in the room was laughing at me, and eventually I joined in when I realised that I was in the camp. I'd never been so grateful to wake up in there.

Anyway, Csaszi said he was heading to Spain, which he'd never been to before. I agreed to join him, because

I'd never been there either and another Hungarian guy joined our company as well.

So three of us headed for Spain. We had some money when we started. The plan was to take the train to Ventimiglia and then the bus to get close to the border and then cross on foot to Menton and take the train from there towards Spain. The problem was that when we arrived at the border by bus, it stopped about five metres from the border, so we couldn't cross secretly. The bus was mainly full of locals who could come and go as they pleased because they had passport. We were right down on the south coast, near Monaco and Nice – the Italian Riviera. That was our preferred crossing point, but we just had to turn around and go back to Italy because we couldn't cross to France without passport. The problem was that all the other passengers from the bus were entering France; we were the only ones turning around and heading towards where we came from. Of course, all the border guards saw us, since we couldn't have been more suspicious.

We got off the bus and walked a few hundred metres until we were out of sight. We crossed the border but we were immediately caught and locked in a holding cell at the border station. Because they saw us not crossing the border, border guards dressed as civilians were looking and waiting for us in Menton. They were not nice. It was October so it was very cold and they didn't even give us a blanket for the night. Then the next day they escorted us to the gate and we were handed over to the Italian authorities.

We went back to Genoa to regroup and spent two nights there until we ran out of money. The third guy quit, so it was just me and Csaszi left. We hatched a plan and decided that we would cross the border hiding in the roof space above the toilets in the train. The roof hatch was easy to open with a pair of pliers from below and you could push it open with your fingers from above and there was enough room there for both of us. That's how we got into France.

CHAPTER THIRTEEN

SWALLOW MY PRIDE

The roof space above the toilet was safe to completely avoid being seen, so we didn't risk leaving our hiding place, even after we had crossed the border. We stayed hidden until the train reached its terminus. We knew the approximate time this should happen, so after the train had been abandoned in the sidings for the night, we waited for half an hour and crawled down – very stiff and dirty. We couldn't have risked crawling down during the journey, because we couldn't guarantee that the toilet door would be closed, so we'd be visible to the other passengers.

The terminus was Nice, so we alighted there. It wasn't close to the border, so we knew that we wouldn't run into any border guards. We were relatively safe, just without any money. We hitchhiked to Toulon, where we broke into a food kiosk and stole some froze pizzas (it was out of season, so there was no other food) and we slept there as well. In the morning we continued our journey and by the night we got to Marseilles. We slept on the beach that night. We couldn't sleep in the park, because it was closed. I was ravenously hungry and really thirsty. I had been told by Csaszi that there was a drinking fountain in the park but nowhere else, so that was very disappointing. We were freezing as well and we were travelling very light so we had no more clothes to put on. We even used our towels as blankets but it didn't help much.

The next day, the park opened and I was able to quench my thirst. We hung out in the park that day and fed ourselves by scavenging leftover sandwiches from the park bins. Better to eat a second hand sandwich than to starve. We didn't want to hang around much longer in Marseilles because we wanted to get to Spain, where we would have accommodation and food as a refugee. So that day we hitchhiked away from Marseilles and reached Montpellier. There was a petrol station there, so we broke into it and stole some food and spent a night there.

From Montpellier, we hitchhiked to Narbonne, 100km to the south-west, where we met some gypsy travellers, seasonal workers from Spain. They offered us some work. They agreed to pay us 50 franks a day each as well as free accommodation and food and then drop us off at the train station afterwards. It wasn't a good deal, the money was poor, but they were subcontracting and we were very hungry so we grabbed the opportunity. It was better than nothing. After all, how difficult could picking grapes be? As you know by now kids, I hardly picked any at school. Very hard as it turned out – and backbreaking. The gypsies were very good to us; they were very friendly and it was fun to live with them. They worked hard and they partied hard. Every night they would have dancing and drinking and still manage to work hard the next day. We stayed with them for about four days and then they finished that area and moved on.

We parted company at this point. They took us back to Narbonne, close to where they had picked us up. Now we had a little bit of money, so we bought train tickets and took the train to Cerbère, a coastal border town and on the other side, was Portbou. We got lucky again, because nobody spotted us crossing the border. We used the same trick of getting off the train before the border and crossing on foot. On the Spanish side, we caught the train to

Barcelona, which was about 180km away.

In Barcelona, we went to the Red Cross to register as refugees. It was October 1987. I stayed in Spain with Csaszi until November 1988 and learned how to speak Spanish. I spoke a bit of Italian, but still needed a Hungarian translator – and he turned out to be a very famous retired Hungarian footballer, Zoltán Czibor. He had played in the fifties and sixties when Hungary was a top international team, so he was very famous. I'm not interested in football, so actually I didn't know him; it was my football-mad refugee friend of mine from Germany, Csaszi, who recognised him.

Zoltán Czibor was one of the many people who left Hungary in the first wave, but now he was in a bad way, a poor guy, an alcoholic living on his own and translating for money. He invited us to his place and we slept there several times and we brought booze so he was always happy to see us. He lived off his reputation. He was so famous that he would walk into shops and tell the shopkeeper he had no money and take what he wanted for free. He also told lots of good stories. He'd had an amazing life when he was younger, with money. He had travelled the world so he'd had lots of rich experiences. He was funny too, with a good sense of humour so we always enjoyed his company.

We didn't stay in camps. The Red Cross housed us in a hotel but we were free to rent any other hotel of our choice. We had 30,000 pezos monthly allowance. Half of that was for the hotel and the rest was for food. Of course, we bought some tinned food and then drank the rest of the allowance within a few weeks. Sometimes we survived on cooked pasta with no sauce, just some salt and pepper. Despite this, three meals a day and not having to fight my drunk father felt like heaven.

Also, my brother's application for refuge had been accepted in Canada so he was now living and working there and would send me $150 every month, which was 15,000 pesos. We shared the money. In groups, we usually pooled our resources. I felt rich. Like every new, young 'millionaire' I started blowing my money on things I wanted, rather than needed. Believe it or not, I sometimes bought clothes too. Mainly I spent my cash on necessities, such as booze and dope! After running through my fortune for the month in a few weeks – I didn't want to stop splurging – I found a business that I figured was a job for life! We found a place where we actually got paid for giving blood. We could do that every week and every fourth week we received an additional cash bonus. So we gave blood every week.

The blood money flowed and so did the wine. But we had to set boundaries for our own good. To make sure that we didn't drink ourselves to death, one night, we formed teams (there were four of us, so each team had two members). We had to compete against each other, but to make sure everybody got some wine, the winning team got double. The challenge involved flicking an olive across the room into your partner's mouth – you miss, you take a drink. You get it in, take two. It was a win-win situation.

I'm not much of an athlete, but even I know that in team sports, you help your mates. So I opened my mouth wide. Missed. Then I opened my mouth wider. Missed again. I opened my mouth even wider, as wide as I could. You know just to help my team. BINGO! Best shot of the night. Winners, losers took their drinks. Good times! Except the next time after trying to catch the olive I realised my mouth was still open and it wouldn't close because my jaw muscles had seized up and my jaw had locked in that open position.

I got a few more olives thrown at me before anybody realised I wasn't playing the game anymore. Since we were all such good friends, nobody stopped laughing or throwing olives, even after they saw what had happened. Eventually, even though it was hilarious, my friends decided to get me professional help. They didn't have to look far. 'Doc' lived just down the corridor. We all knew him and that he was a qualified medic (or so we thought). How else could he afford such attire otherwise? His wife beater (tank top) and underwear had barely any stains on them more than a few weeks old. 'Doc' was hairy and sweaty, but he apparently knew what to do – he put my head under his armpit and squeezed hard enough for me to taste the smell of his sweat, but he didn't succeed. The pain was excruciating.

'You need a real doctor here!' he exclaimed. Later, we learned that his nickname came from his favourite character from Bugs Bunny: 'What's up, doc?'

We hailed a taxi and raced to the hospital. We got there without trouble. 'What's the problem? How can I help?' asked the 'real' doctor. Simple questions for those who speak Spanish. Unfortunately, though, my friend couldn't, I could: 'Awaw a awawaw aw awaw' I told him in fluent Spanish. He looked at me as if I was speaking Martian. So I repeated it. 'Awaw a awawaw aw awaw'. He must have been speaking a different dialect because he still didn't understand me. Then he spoke English. Luckily, my friend spoke enough English to get me into an examination room. However, the stench of the hospital, plus the booze I'd been pouring down myself all night and the pain in my jaw led to me feeling really woozy. Just as one of the doctors was examining me, I had to lunge up from the bed and grab a wastebasket to be sick in with my jaw locked open!

If that wasn't bad enough, I then felt my bowels begin to tremble and had to dash to the toilet with the wastebasket in my hand. I spent ages in there, puking and shitting. Eventually, my body was empty and it stopped, so I cleaned myself up and tried to rinse my mouth with water, although it was very hard to do with my jaw locked wide open.

I finally made it back into the room where the doctor gave me a shot to relax my jaw muscles and put a bandage around my head. I was supposed to rest there for a few hours, but I got bored, so, after whistling to my friend outside to tell him where I was, I tore the bandage off and leapt out of the window.

My friend and I started to walk home, thinking in our boozed-up state that our motel was close by except it wasn't. It was very late at night and I was exhausted from drinking and all the drama of the evening, so I yawned and my jaw locked open again. We trudged back to the hospital and I was treated by the same two doctors as before. I was surprised that they weren't angry with me for leaving earlier and getting back into that state, but I think they were maybe in shock as their own jaws dropped open as wide as mine when they saw me again. I don't think they'd seen a case like me before and probably not again since. However, this time they bandaged my head up almost totally, leaving just a space for my eyes and a slit at my mouth. They told me I needed to leave this on for at least twenty-four hours, only eating what I could take through a straw. Soon enough, I recovered, took off my mummy mask and was back to my old tricks, but I will never forget that terrible night I got lockjaw.

CHAPTER FOURTEEN

HAIR OF THE DOG

Next, I found out that two best friends of mine from Hungary, Tigi and Szkuri, were living in Madrid, so I bought a ticket and went there. I couldn't stay long because I had to be back in Barcelona to collect my monthly allowance from the Red Cross. Then I couldn't buy a ticket to back Barcelona because I spent all my money in Madrid.

Tigi, me & Szkury in Madrid being happy after a bottle of vodka

So even though I wasn't crossing any borders, I still had to travel in a roof space above the toilet just to get to Barcelona in time for my monthly allowance. As soon as

I picked the money up I headed back to Madrid with a plan to invite my friends back with me to Barcelona and show them how much better the life was over there.

Barcelona was much more fun than Madrid, which was just a hot city with no beach. Madrid wasn't much fun: we drank, we ran out of money. It was very hard to steal in Spain but we had no other choice in Madrid because there was no 'blood money'. The stores had lots of cameras and dozens of store detectives disguised as shoppers, so the odds were stacked against us. However, there were so many shoplifters in Spain that the police were rarely called so if we were caught, we only really risked being banned from that store. We were ejected from some stores three or four times without being arrested. We mostly stole booze but since that was one of the most commonly stolen items, there was at least one camera just watching that section. We couldn't be subtle there. We just walked in, each one of us grabbed some kind of hard liquor, put it under our jackets and made our way out of the store hoping that at least one of us would get lucky. It worked most of the time.

Fortunately, there were other ways to get alcohol. One of them was watching the trucks delivering booze to shops or pubs. When the guy went in with the delivery, we ran to the truck, grabbed as many bottles as we could and ran away. We never got caught doing that.

The other method was stealing from inside a pub. One time, we were drinking in a pub. When we went down to the basement to use the toilet, we noticed that the wine was right beside it in an open storage area. So before we left we always used the loo and then grabbed a few bottle of wine. Of course, after the fourth or fifth time, the owner figured out what we were doing and the police were waiting for us at the front of the pub. So we were banned from there too. Again, no consequences, so no big deal really.

We didn't always steal wine. Sometimes we even paid for it. We found a place that sold very cheap, very shitty wine; I remember it was cheaper even than the Coke. In Madrid we were living in a hotel called Pension Altara on Calle de Atocha. Three of us shared one room, the toilet and shower in the hallway was for everybody and we even had to pay for hot water. Except for us, that hotel housed many ordinary hard working people. To get the cheap wine we had to bring our own containers. Whenever we got drunk we used to listen to music late and it was quite loud. But we were mindful of the workers, so it wasn't obnoxiously loud. The workers tolerated us and knew our routine, so when they saw us leaving with four two-litre empty plastic Coke bottles, the poor souls knew we'd be up all night making noise.

We could get fed from food banks, collecting sandwiches, but then we had to wake up very early. We knew which churches gave out sandwiches so we visited as many as we could before they closed, so we would have enough for dinner too. There was one church where we could have lunch but it was mainly beans, lentils and chickpeas with not much variety, the same food every day, depending on what they had received in donations. The best days were the Spanish holidays because then we got paella. And luckily, the Spanish had lots of holidays. Every fortnight they seemed to be celebrating something. I loved that in the Spanish people. There would be lots of people on the street, music, singing, dancing and of course, fireworks. But this hand-to-mouth existence was no fun, so my friends Tigi and Szkuri agreed to come to Barcelona with me.

Me, Tigi and Szkuri finally getting drunk in Barcelona, ohh, and
playing pool too

Las Ramblas is the name of the famous boulevard
which runs through the heart of Barcelona's city centre.
At that time it was always buzzing with activity including
lots of drug dealers and prostitutes. At one time we lived
in a very shitty motel called Pension Tolosa just off this
street on Carrer d'en Xucla, in part of the red light district.

There was a pub we frequently visited and one day we
met a guy there from Marrakech, Morocco who was
selling drugs. Quickly, he became our drug dealer and we
became good friends. He had a lots of stories to tell and
we had a lots of stories too. He told us that dealing drugs
was very competitive and dangerous in Barcelona, so he
always carried a small axe inside his jacket.

Sometimes we had visitors from other countries but
usually they only stayed for a few weeks, just like my
brother, Reaper and I went to Vienna, Austria to visit our
friends. These guys never stayed long and didn't register
as refugees.

Our first visitors were actually from Vienna. We didn't
know them but we had a mutual friend and that was
enough to welcome them. There was a nice girl with them
called Suzy. She had a boyfriend but for some reason he

stayed in Vienna. We showed them around, took them sightseeing and to the beach where we spent most of our time. One night we took them to our favourite pub to drink and buy some drugs. As usual, I was drinking heavily. One minute I was in the pub, the next minute I was in a stairway of a building having sex with Suzy. I was so happy that at least once when I came to my senses I wasn't in custody or jail.

Another time a guy came to visit Csaszi and he was driving a Renault Fuego. When he ran out of money he sold the car to us and our time in the Costa Brava improved considerably. We could easily get around in the small towns and find the best place to party. Our favourite towns were Lloret de Mar and Calella. We had so much fun there that we gave up our accommodation and spent all our money there and slept on the beach until the next allowance day.

With our next allowance, we rented a hotel again just to get a little bit more comfortable for a while. The hotel was called Pension Cristina and it was on Carrer de Tamarit. It was more comfortable but a lot less fun. After paying the rent we didn't have much left for pubs so we mostly partied at the hotel. The owner warned us a few times that our behaviour was unacceptable but we didn't care much. After a few weeks he kicked us out, so we went back to the Costa Brava.

In Calella we ran out of money so we stole two handbags from a couple of tourists. We got away and met up with our friends on the beach. We knew that we needed to leave town quickly because the police would be looking for us, but our friends were in no hurry to leave. They were still drinking and swimming in the sea after night fall, despite the urgency. We begged them but still they didn't want to leave. It wasn't long before the police arrived. I got arrested with Szkuri who hadn't been involved. He just had short hair like me and was picked out from a lineup. I told Szkuri that he should give up the other guy and I'll also tell the police that it was him but he didn't listen to me.

We spent a few days in the local lock up and then we were transferred to the jail in Lloret de Mar. Szkuri had an earring that one of the other prisoners liked. There were four of them and two of us. It was a simple earring and one of them said, 'I like it – you give it to me?' My friend Szkuri said 'No.' 'Why did you say that?' I asked. 'Why didn't you just give it to him? Now they will beat us up.' They took it from him by force, but they didn't beat us up. In fact, we sort of became friends after that.

Shortly afterwards, those same guys advised us to cut our veins so that we would be taken to the hospital, where our handcuffs would be removed and then we could run away. So we cut our veins to make them bleed and off we went to the hospital, but even as the nurse was doing the stitches, we remained handcuffed, so there was no possibility of escape. I still have the scar today. So that was a waste of time.

Three days later, we were found guilty and transferred to jail in Barcelona for 45 days. Szkuri was younger than me so he was transferred to a juvie and I went to a normal jail for adults. That was a scary jail full of rough people and there were gang problems too. I was in isolation for a day or so when I first arrived in Barcelona prison. I got given a small hygiene pack with soap, toothpaste, disposable razor and it also contained condoms which made me worried, as there were no women in the prison. It wasn't like the prison in Austria. The first thing I did was to take the blade from the razor just in case I had to defend myself.

I soon discovered that a fellow refugee, our drug dealer from Marrakech, was already in the prison. I had been put in a jail cell by then, but the jail in Barcelona was different to any other prison I'd been in or heard of. Prisoners could move around freely during the day, the doors were open and they could go to any cell if there was a free bed. So I was able to move to his cell and spend my sentence there. He and his friends were dealing drugs even inside, so they shared some with me and they also protected me.

Szkuri and I got let out at the same time, a Friday night and we met up at the seaside and slept on a bench. The next day we met up with the guy who stole the bags with me but didn't go to jail. He was supposed to have visited us in jail to bring us money and food because Szkuri had gone to jail on his behalf, but he never did any of that. In fact, in the meantime he allowed others to steal our stuff. By the time I was released, all I had was a cheque from my brother for $150, but it was a weekend so I couldn't cash it. So the guy allowed us to sneak into his hotel and sleep there. However, he got into a fight with his girlfriend and the police were called and we got thrown out, so we had to sleep on the beach over the weekend until I could cash my cheque on the Monday.

Me, leaving Barcelona totally sober and sad (maybe because I was sober)

On Monday we cashed my cheque and went to the Red Cross to pick up our allowance. They told us that this was our last but one payment. We were welcome to stay if we could support and legalise ourselves but they don't help us anymore. So we decided to leave. The next destination was Germany because they would still offer refugees support, but on the way we wanted to stop in Rome and Vienna to visit old friends.

CHAPTER FIFTEEN

SOMEBODY LIKE ME

We left Spain at the end of November 1988 and we went first to Rome. I was 21 years old by this point. I was just living day by day. But I was free. Even though I was broke, travelling without any valid ID or passport and living in the refugee system, it was like an extended European gap year. You know kids, I never dreamed I'd be able to go and visit the places I had been. Plus I had a ten year jail sentence waiting for me in Hungary.

Thanks to my brother's cheque, we were able to buy tickets from Barcelona to the last border stop before Italy, which was Portbou, where we got off the train and then walked across the border. In two days we reached Monaco. It was end of November but everything was so shiny, as if they cleaned up the whole town every day and there were so many expensive cars. I never seen anything like this before.

Then we walked more than four hours to Ventimiglia and from there we took a train to Sanremo, where we put our luggage in storage locker and went to Imperia and told the police that our stuff had been stolen, so they gave us a free ticket to Rome, so that we could get a temporary passport from the Hungarian Embassy. But our stuff was not stolen, just in the storage locker. So we went back to the locker, picked up our luggage and travelled for free to Rome. We met our friends and drank together through the night, but we didn't stay long.

Finally getting drunk (or already drunk) in Rome again

We moved on the next day. We didn't really have a plan. We were heading to Vienna first to visit other friends and then to Germany and that was it.

So we left for Vienna. Our friends locked us up in the roof space above the toilet again, from Rome to Vienna, it was a long way. We had to sneak out a few times to use the toilet. We had to listen, then when no one was around, one of us would jump down and quickly lock the door. We both did our business and then climbed back into the roof space. We spent more than 15 hours making that train journey. We left in the late afternoon and we got to Vienna the following morning and they don't serve any food above those toilets!

We had to be very quiet whenever someone used the toilet. There was only space for the two of us and a small backpack each. We couldn't lie on the door because that was the weak point, and we could have fallen through. Imagine the scene kids that would have caused! There were electric cables and plumbing for the toilet to keep us company. It was a maintenance hatch. But it became our home for 15 hours.

We finally arrived in Vienna and tracked down a few

friends. We walked into a city that was preparing for Christmas. It was supposed to be a flying one-day visit, but life was good there so we stayed longer than planned. It was easy to shoplift and make money again, the same way that we had done it before. It was a different bunch of people, but almost the same methods. We stayed there for about three months.

The Hungarian 'underground' had become more developed by then. We were sharing information about stores that were easy to steal from and places where we could sell the goods. It was even easier to make money than the first time I was there. Now we were selling stolen goods to Austrian shop owners and not just on Mariahilfer Straße but all over Vienna. They also ordered goods just like Hungarians so our 'network' got a lot bigger.

Once we went to a Hungarian party where I met Árpi again. At first I didn't immediately recognise him. It was only after I heard him speak (he has a very distinctive way of speaking) than I realised that he was the guy who had saved my hair and let me spend a night at his parents' flat in Budapest.

I introduced myself 'Árpi, it's me, Zoltán. Do you remember? You saved me from having my head shaved? In Budapest'. Árpi stared at me blankly. For a moment I thought he might head-butt me, then he smiled the biggest smile and shouted: 'Zoltán, Fuck me mate! How are you? How's life with you?' And this chance second meeting was the beginning of a great friendship.

Árpi had a girlfriend at that time and they were living in a hotel near Amstetten. They were just visiting friends in Vienna. We were drinking and talking all night and met up afterwards as often as we could. He was still a skinhead and I was a skinhead as well, we liked the same music and clothing but he was much tougher than me.

One afternoon I was selling stolen goods to Hungarians working on Mariahilfer Straße when one of them told me that Árpi was in Vienna again and where I could find him. Those guys working on Mariahilfer Straße were our 'mobiles'. We were on that street at least once or twice a day so we left messages with them and when they saw the guy the message was for, they just told him. That's how we communicated with each other because there were no mobile phones then. That was our network. Can you kids imagine the word without mobile phones? I don't think so.

So I went to see Árpi. He was sad and upset because his girlfriend left him for another Hungarian guy we knew very well. He was also stealing goods but with a different group of Hungarians. We knew each other because we shared the same 'trade'. Since we partied many times together and shared information on the street, we knew where that guy lived so we went to pay him a visit. I knew it was not going to end well but I went with Árpi for emotional support. The group was four guys but I knew that Árpi could easily take all of them by himself, so I wasn't there to fight. Actually, one of the guys was Suzy's boyfriend. Kids, do you remember Suzy from 'Stairway to Haven' in Barcelona, right? I still remembered her and she remembered me too. It wasn't just stairwell sex, we liked each other too.

Anyway kids, let's get back to Árpi. Árpi kicked the door in. One of the guys got up from the sofa and made his way towards Árpi to calm him down. Wrong move. Árpi kicked him in the chest so hard that the guy flew a few metres back to the sofa. Árpi didn't even have a beef with him. Imagine the look on the face of the guy Árpi came for. After that kick the rest of the group stayed where they were. They were so scared they didn't move a muscle. I was so glad that I was on Árpi's side. The other guys were not hurt, they sorted the thing out without more violence. Árpi didn't steal goods and he was afraid that this new boyfriend would include his ex-girlfriend in his 'daily routine' and that when they got caught, she would go to jail too. Actually, I think that was what happened. They got caught stealing, were thrown into jail and got sent back to Hungary, but by then Árpi didn't care about her anymore.

Árpi stayed for a little while and we tried to ease his pain with lots of drinking. As I mentioned earlier, in Hungary, skinheads and punks were friendly with each other but not in Vienna. I told Árpi that a few of them had chased me once so now I had to be careful not to run into them. Árpi had a different idea and asked me to find them. I knew exactly where they usually hung out so I went there with Árpi and luckily they were there. Without saying a word, Árpi head-butted the first one, kicked a second one in the chest and punched the third one square in the face. In seconds all of them were on the ground. Árpi kicked them a few times and told them that if they ever did anything to me again, he would come here every day and kick their asses. After that I never had a problem with the Viennese punks.

On that weekend we went to a concert too. I can't remember who was playing because we only stayed for probably 15–20 minutes before we were thrown out. When we arrived I suggested to Árpi that we all reach the front because that was my favourite spot and I always saw and enjoyed gigs best from there. There was a huge crowd so it was hard and slow to get to the front, so Árpi speeded things up. He head-butted every guy in front of us, which speeded our progress no end, but it quickly alerted the bouncers, so by the time we got to the front they were waiting there to throw us out. It was always fun going out with Árpi.

Sometimes we would be able to travel outside Vienna, if we could find or even hire someone with a car. My refugee friend from Szeged owned a large Mercedes and at first he had made a good living just being a driver, before he moved onto stealing. He could fit lots of stolen merchandise in his trunk, and he could drive people to places where their faces were unknown, which usually meant other big cities. The bigger the shop, generally, the easier it was to steal from, despite security guards, because the ratio of staff to floor area was worse.

I remember kids, one time I stole a toy gun that looked real and I put it in front of me on the dashboard. My window was open and during a sudden left turn, the gun flew out of the window. 'Luckily', it happened near to a bus stop so people were staring. My friend quickly stopped the car, I jumped out, grabbed the gun, rushed back to the car and we were burning rubber and sped off with smoking tyres. I can imagine what those people were thinking. Young guy jumping out of a big Mercedes to grab his gun – they probably thought that I was some kind of 'big shot', a hard criminal or a 'mafioso'.

I didn't just stay in Vienna, I went to other smaller towns to visit friends. And yes, I visited Árpi too in his hotel near Amstetten. We went to visit his friends in Amstetten and we got drunk, of course, and we started shouting 'Sieg Heil' in the street and drawing swastikas on the hoods of cars in the snow, so we got arrested. I had no ID card or passport, I was illegally in the country. You remember kids, I'd been arrested in Austria before and then I was banned from the country. As soon as they checked my name in their system they knew I shouldn't be in Austria so they put me in a holding cell right away. The next day they transferred me to St. Pölten to the jail. They wanted to send me back to Hungary. I learned that from other Hungarians in the jail – let me tell you kids, you can find Hungarians everywhere.

The Hungarians told me to start a hunger strike. They said if I did it for ten days I'd be thrown out of jail. After ten days I would need medical attention and the authorities wouldn't spend money on me. But ten days was also not sufficient time to process all the paperwork so that they could transport me back to Hungary. So I started a hunger strike on 21st January 1989 and it worked. On 1st February they let me go, so I went back to Vienna to find my friends.

I met up with my friends in Vienna and we were partying again. A few days after my release from St Pölten jail, Szkuri went into a store instead of me because I had a bad feeling and they caught him for stealing and threw him in jail. Not even two weeks later after a party I was walking home an Austrian girl I liked very much, when the police stopped us and asked for ID cards. Of course, I still didn't have any, so I was arrested again and jailed in Vienna. I found some Hungarian guys in there too and they told me that Szkuri was actually sent back to Hungary. The way to get out of that jail, so I was advised by fellow inmates, was to swallow something metal like a piece of cutlery, and then get sent to hospital. Once the metal object had been detected with an X-ray, I would be released because no one wanted to take responsibility if the foreign object perforating my stomach whilst I was in their custody. But I didn't have a spoon, or anything metal, so I took two zippers from my bomber jacket, secured them together so they looked bigger and swallowed them.

The guards X-rayed me, but told me that they weren't going to let me go, just because of that. So I had to start the hunger strike again, and that worked. They let me go after ten days.

I hadn't eaten for 21 days out of the previous 35 days. Fasting wasn't easy, but after the first few days, you stop feeling ravenously hungry, as long as you drink plenty of fluids. The first three days were always the hardest, especially when I was sharing a cell with a group of guys who were eating and trying to encourage me to have some food. It was nasty prison food, but it still seemed like a banquet when you were hungry.

Every other day the guards took me to the sick bay to get checked over and weighed by a doctor. On the tenth day, he warned the guards that they would need to either send me to hospital or release me, so they released me. Can you imagine kids how skinny I was by the time I got out? I was so skinny I could pull my jeans down without undoing the buttons.

I've since learned that, as long as you don't exceed the ten days and you're careful about how you reintroduce food, fasting is actually very healthy. When your body is burning fat as fuel, and isn't expending energy on digestion, it can focus more on healing damaged cells throughout the body. The body also produces more anti-oxidants so that after fasting ends, it's better protected against damage from free radicals.

Our hunter-gatherer ancestors would have been very familiar with fasting in between periods of plenty, so even though I was skinny when I left prison, the detox benefits meant I was probably in better shape than if I had spent the time getting drunk. Everyone's fasting now. Come to think of it, with my 'Hungarian Refugee Prison Fasting Diet', I was decades ahead of my time!

CHAPTER SEXTEEN

A REAL COOL TIME

As soon as I was released I went to my friend's place who was renting a flat in Vienna. Tigi who had come over from Germany and another very good friend of mine from Hungary was there too: Imi – whose son, Kristóf, is my godson now. What a pleasant surprise. We were very happy and had to celebrate so we drank all night and spent the night there. They were planning to set off for Germany the next day, so I joined them.

Tigi was living in Überlingen, a German city on the northern shore of Obersee Bodensee (Lake Constance) in Baden-Württemberg near the border with Switzerland, so we planned to head there first.

This was before mobile phones, but it was easy enough to find friends, because I'd just go to the places where we used to hang out, or go to the streets where I thought they might be shoplifting.

If we wanted to go to a different country we had some maps to help our journeys, but not always, because often we would have to rely on the person we had just met up with and hoped that they will be able to find their way back to where they had just come from. But on this occasion we were lucky because we had Tigi who knew the way to his home.

We used to write letters to each other, so we'd invariably have addresses on the letters that we could visit or we could call a friend who was living in a hotel to meet us at a certain time at the train station. A lots of my friends weren't nomadic like me, they were much more rooted in one place, they had jobs and they stayed put, so they were usually fairly easy to find.

Once they had registered in the refugee system, my friends were housed by the authorities in a hotel or other lodgings, just like I had been and they stayed there until it was their turn to be permanently settled in Canada, the States or Australia. All I had to do was to find one of them, and because we all knew each other, that single contact would be enough to locate other friends, especially in Vienna because they all congregated in the same few places. If anyone came from another town or country, they would pass on information to these settled people, so they became the repository for this information. It was our own personal tourist/refugee underground grapevine. We represented an entire network of people living outside of society and mostly we were all friendly.

My & Tigi, 'Deutschland, Deutschland Über Alles'

So kids, the next stop was Germany, with Tigi and Imi. I wanted to go somewhere safe, I didn't want to get sent to prison again and have to do another hunger strike. We bought a train ticket and headed for Überlingen. We got off just before the border, as usual, and crossed by foot. I was so weak from the hunger strikes that Tigi and Imi had to carry my travel bag. We stayed in Überlingen for a week, then we headed for Freiburg, where we wanted to register as a refugee.

In that week, Árpi joined us too. He has some German background so he was planning to get German citizenship. When we got to Freiburg, Imi and I were sent to a homeless shelter for the night but Árpi was accommodated in a hotel because of his German background. The homeless shelter stank so much that we had to apply aftershave balm under our noses every ten minutes.

We hardly slept and in the morning we slipped away without breakfast as soon as they opened the doors. It was so sad that Imi changed his mind and didn't register with me as a refugee. Then I was sent alone to the closest refugee camp, which was at Karlsruhe. I stayed there for a while until the paperwork was done, and then they sent me to Heilbronn, another camp, about 55km north of Stuttgart. That was my official accommodation until I left Germany. As usual, I hardly stayed in the camp, preferring to stay with my friends. There were some Hungarian guys there but I didn't have much in-common with them, so I didn't hang out with them. I stayed in Germany from February 1989 and left in September.

In Germany, stealing was easy, just like in Austria but selling the stolen goods was a lot harder. We didn't have that Hungarian 'network' there. But in Germany we could steal cigarettes and those were easy to sell in the camp and to other Hungarians. There were lots of cigarette machines on the streets and we figured out how to empty them. With a wire bent into an 'L' shape, we could reach up to the cigarettes from the bottom slot where they should have come out. We poked the smaller part of the 'L' shape through the cigarette box and pulled them out. Of course, this was a 'night job' when the police were more active, so we had to hide the bags full of cigarettes in case we were stopped and searched. The next day, when the streets were busy and we were not suspicious, we would go back to retrieve the bags.

Of course, the safe way to make money was working. In Überlingen, even Tigi worked. When I stayed with him, he would go off to work in the morning and I would wake up later and stroll into town. We had our favourite pub, so I usually ended up there and would drink and eat until Tigi finished for the day and could join me. Because I didn't have money at the end, before we left for his hotel, he had to pay my bill as well. He was a nice guy and still is.

Heilbronn was a small and friendly city (smaller than Szeged) and because I was a skinhead, I made a few more skinhead friends there – two skinhead girls at first, one of them became my girlfriend while I was there – they talked to me because I was the new skinhead in town. They had a party that night so they invited me. Everybody was very friendly, even though skinheads don't generally like refugees, but I was fine. I knew enough German by this time to be able to talk to them and make friends. You know kids, I'm a friendly motherfucker.

It was on this visit to Germany that I was told about the double-withdrawal bank scam. This was 1989, so when you made a withdrawal from your bank account, it wasn't a computerised network and therefore it didn't instantly update your digital account, so it was possible to withdraw some money from one branch and then in 30 minutes, withdraw some more money from another branch nearby, even if you had cleared out your account during the first visit. But you needed paperwork to do that, so some guys told me that if I did this scam for them, it would ruin my name, but then they would in return give me a German passport and pay for my journey to Toronto, Canada.

I was eager to leave Western Europe at this point because the Berlin Wall was about to fall, my brother was in Canada and I was ready to settle down over there, so I agreed. These guys had DM7,500 for the scam. All I had to do was to open a bank account, deposit the money and withdraw it twice. My refugee ID was sufficient to open a bank account. I went along with it and did the crime for them, but then they double crossed me about getting my German passport and the flight to Canada. They kept stringing me along and making excuses, day after day, so in the end I had to get one of my friends, Péter, who was a foot taller than me – a big scary angry guy – to pay them a visit.

I had to get out of the country quickly because sooner or later I was going to get arrested for that bank crime. Péter phoned them up and got very heavy with them and told them that he was going to come round the next day and so they got scared. The next day we went to meet them and they gave me the passport and some money – not enough to buy a ticket, but I spoke to my brother and he said he could get me a ticket from Paris to Toronto. I didn't want to fly from Germany with my German passport because the moment I spoke to anyone, they would know I wasn't German, so it made more sense to fly from France instead.

Péter rented me a room in a hotel somewhere outside of Stuttgart, so my name wasn't in the guest book, and then he went back to Tübingen. I should have kept a low profile until my brother had taken care of the ticket but you should know kids by now that I'm a fuck-up. The first night I was still buzzing with excitement from the day's events, but that feeling was gone by the next night. So I decided to go to the pub nearby. I was bored by myself so I made friends at the pub. We were drinking and having fun together and I even paid for a few rounds.

When I got drunk enough, instead of paying my bill, I

jumped through the toilet window and went back to my hotel. In the morning I was woken by a loud bang on my door. I had a very bad hangover but I managed to open the door to see two policemen standing outside. The hangover disappeared in an instant and was replaced by fear. They asked for my ID and told me that they were here because I 'forgot' to pay my bill the previous evening. Unfortunately, I had told the guys I had been drinking with the name of the hotel where I was staying. The guys must have told the bartender, who told the police and that's how they found me. I told them that I was very drunk and that nothing like this had happened to me before. They checked my ID card; nothing was wrong with it so they give me a warning and asked me to pay my bill. I gave them the money and they left.

That was such a close call. By now I was literally shaking with fear, so I phoned Péter and asked him to come and pick me up. He came as soon as he could and I stayed with him until I left Germany.

Now I needed to get from Germany to Paris. This time Péter simply drove us across the border, with his and my passport on the dashboard. Péter was Hungarian but he got the German citizenship because of his German background so he had German passport and he spoke fluent German too. They only stopped on average about one in every twenty cars, so my odds were good, but I was so nervous, much more scared than I had been when crossing secretly on foot. Not to mention, the German passport was an original one with the owner's picture and name in it. I had to grow my hair and comb it backwards with some hair gel on to look more like him. Fortunately, they didn't stop us, they just waved us through.

Péter then drove me to Strasburg in French and I bought a ticket from there to Paris. I spent a night in Paris but I didn't sleep even though my plane to Canada left the next day. I walked around all night seeing the sights! I saw the Eiffel Tower, the Champs-Élysées, the Arc de Triomphe and Notre-Dame. It was magical. When I was there with you, Mirella, it wasn't so magical. Paris was dirty, with lots of tourists everywhere and pushy people selling souvenirs at every tourist attraction. Until I told them to 'Fuck off,' we couldn't get rid of them. But I still had a wonderful time with you, Mirella.

CHAPTER SEVENTEEN

THE JOB THAT ATE MY BRAIN

So there I was at Paris airport – a Hungarian refugee facing ten years in prison if extradited from there or from Canada to Hungary. I'd been on the run, from one refugee camp to another using multiple different identities and passports and I'd been arrested several times. I'd spent time in several jails. I'd done two hunger strikes. I had cut my veins and, lacking a spoon, I had swallowed a zipper, to no avail. I'd become so skinny I probably looked malnourished. I was a skinhead but not a violent one, even though I'd been befriended by a lots of people.

I had few employable skills on paper. I had no resume. I didn't even speak English in those days. I had less than $100 in my pocket. I don't even think I had a wallet.

I had to go into the office to pick up the ticket. I looked up in my dictionary: 'I got one ticket here'. That was it. That was the extent of my English. But they understood. They asked for my passport (under the name of B. Volker), I showed it to them and they gave me my ticket.

I was supposed to land in Toronto on 9th September 1989 and my brother was supposed to meet me there. I was very excited, because not only was I going to see my brother again for the first time in a few years – the last time we had parted company was in Rome – I was landing on his actual birthday. It was perfect timing. Then the captain announced over the tannoy that we were going to be delayed because of bad weather and would have to land somewhere else. I was very sad and upset. Finally, after we had circled for a while in the air, the weather changed and we were able to land in Toronto after all.

Going through customs I was very nervous because I was so close. The customs official asked me a question in English, so I asked if he could speak to me in German instead. He asked me some very simple questions and I explained that I had friends waiting for me (I couldn't say one of them was my brother, because our passports had different names: he was Mihály and I was Volker). They didn't check how much money I had. If they had, they would have had to phone my 'friend' to vouch that they would be supporting me.

The one thing I could control was my clothing. You can't have the luxury of being scruffy when you are sneaking into a country on a fake passport. I wasn't dressed as a skinhead, that was for sure. I was wearing a good long sleeved collared shirt, a tidy pair of jeans, a pair of brogues. Inside my rucksack was my bomber jacket, my bovver boots and a toothbrush.

When they finally let me through it was a big relief. My brother and two of his friends were waiting anxiously for me. One of them was Reaper from Italy, you remember kids, the guy that I entered Austria with for the first time, who had come down from Montreal to Toronto for a few days because he knew I was arriving. The other was Miki who was Reaper's friend in Montreal but moved to Toronto. My brother and I didn't meet him before but we became very good friends.

We all took a taxi into the town and started celebrating in some of the bars. It was party time! This was my final destination. You know kids, I was thinking that I stretched my freedom as long as I could but it was over now. I was finally going to settle down, get a job and support myself. That was the plan but I got arrested again for attempting to steal a car. I didn't want to do it, but Reaper was insistent. He tried to break into a car using a screwdriver, without success, so we left. Unfortunately, some bystanders had spotted us so they called the police. We were walking home and the police pulled up in their car and took us to the police station to question us. They even showed us evidence which we had apparently left at the crime scene – a wire coat hanger. Planted evidence. You see kids, you can't even trust the police.

I was the only one of my friends to get arrested and had to spend a night in the cell; all the others had Canadian papers, so they were allowed to leave. I was always unlucky with these kind of things although I always managed to get out of prison in a relatively short time. I told the guys not to do it and I explained that I didn't want to do any criminal activities, having just arrived in Canada and yet here I was in trouble again.

The next day I was transferred to Toronto jail. My problem was, I had a German passport, so I had to invent an elaborate story about my brother being my half brother, with a different surname to me, because my mother had separated from my German father shortly after I was born and then conceived my brother with another man. I had grown up in Hungary with my mother so even though I had a German passport after my father, my German was non-existent and I spoke fluent Hungarian, so I would need a Hungarian translator instead of a German one. Luckily, they bought my story so I got a Hungarian translator and could even talk to my brother too. Two days after my brother's birthday and $750 bail later I was released and I became a free man again.

This time, my case actually went to trial and it looked almost certain that I was going to be deported back to Germany, where of course I would be arrested for having someone else's passport, so I didn't turn up to court, which meant that I could no longer use the German passport, because now there was a warrant out for my arrest on that name for skipping trial. From then on I used my brother's driving licence for identification, which had my photograph on it. I went to the Ministry of Transportation office and posed as my brother and I asked for a new driving licence because my brother had a short hair on the picture and I had long hair (because of my German passport). As you know kids, my brother and I very similar looking so they believed that that was my driving licence with short hair so they took my picture with long hair and gave me a new driving licence. Then my brother pretended that he had lost his driving licence and applied for a replacement. Finally, everything got cleared up when my brother took the rap for me and made a statement saying that he was the one who had tried to break into the car.

My brother, me & Reaper at Niagara Falls celebrating my freedom

There was a huge Hungarian community in Toronto when I arrived there but it got smaller and smaller every year until it almost disappeared. There were Hungarian dinner parties for occasions like Easter and Christmas but there were dinner parties just to party.

I think, kids, what I'm about to tell you happened at an Easter dinner party. I can't remember exactly how many of us went to that party but I remember that my brother and Miki were there too. We dressed up nicely and showed up at the party in time for dinner. Every group had a separate table so we got our own as well. We were having fun. The food was great and there was pálinka too. After dinner they changed the Hungarian folk music to music for younger people so we could dance and breathe some life in the room.

There were some young people but most of the guests were old. Lots of them had fled from the 1956 Hungarian revolution but I don't think any of them participated in it; they just came to Toronto looking for a better life. Nothing wrong with that. At that time Canada needed people so badly that they were giving these people lands for free so they would cultivate it. Of course, these lazy bastards didn't want to work hard so they just kept the land and found some easy jobs in Toronto. And in time Toronto grew big and reached their lands. But Toronto was still growing so they bought the lands back – what they had given them for free – for millions. And that is how these idiots made their money. It was just luck. Not hard work, not intelligence, just plain luck. It still wouldn't have been a problem but they thought so much of themselves as if they were more intelligent and above us and we were just worms and that was the problem with them. Most of them couldn't even speak English after being in Canada for over 30 years. Many of them were the worst kind of alcoholic. If someone looked down on anyone it should have been us looking down on them.

I worked as a driver for a guy who had lost his licence for DUI. On one occasion, when he was talking to the owner of the store about the job, the owner asked me if I understood what he was saying. I told the owner: 'He is trying to speak English, so I only understand as much as you'. After that I was his translator as well.

Anyway, let's get back to the party. We were having fun and at the next table a girl started looking at me and when I looked back she always smiled. She was sitting with her grandparents, parents and brother I think. It looked that way because of their age. After a bit of eyeballing, even though I hate dancing, I went to their table and asked her if she wanted to dance with me. But instead of her answering me, the father and the grandfather started giving me shit like I had done something wrong. They told me to leave her alone and go back to my table and asked me, what the hell I was thinking, asking her to dance. I didn't see that coming. So kids, I told them that I was asking and talking nicely so far, but if that was the way people talked to each other here then 'Fuck you, you fucking old farts, you twats, you stupid wankers…' I was about halfway through when the brother jumped up and pushed me. I still remember how my brother's face lit up right away. He was just waiting for this moment. He jumped up too and knocked the guy out. After that every man from both tables jumped up and started fighting. Fortunately, we were younger and stronger than them so we knocked them out one by one by the time the staff got to us. They were fair because they threw everybody out from both tables. You see kids, now that is how Hungarians have fun. But still, that was the first and last time I went to a Hungarian dinner party.

Nightmare before Pizza Pizza

I had to get a job. My brother was working as a manager in a fast food pizza restaurant called Pizza Pizza, so he got me a job there. I hated it. The restaurant owner asked me if I wanted to learn English quickly or slowly. I said quickly, so he put me front of house, serving the customers. That was so difficult, taking people's orders because my English was non-existent. Taking orders involved lots of impatient gesturing and pointing at the menu and many exasperated customers.

It was especially difficult when people ordered cigarettes, because I didn't smoke and I was clueless. Lot more pointing was required to get people their precious cigarettes.

My brother gave me a crash course – pointing at pictures and telling me the names for everything. Extra toppings? Forget it! I had to learn all these strange words like 'pepperoni', 'slice', 'extra mushrooms', 'no onions'. It was crazy. Pointing and smiling all day. I must have looked like an idiot.

Lots of kids used to come into the restaurant after school and they used to laugh at me. I didn't know what they were saying but I knew they were making fun of me. When my brother was there, he would tell them to 'fuck off' because he spoke fluent English by then. I also worked at night. At that time pubs would stay open until two in the morning, so we attracted lots of drunk people. The drunk guys were usually fine, but the drunk girls were worse than the kids – they were very rude and I hated them more than the children. I wasn't being paid nearly enough to be humiliated every day by kids and drunks. Suddenly, ten years in prison in Hungary didn't seem so bad.

While I was in Canada I applied to the Hungarian consulate for a pardon, so that I could return to Hungary at some point in the future without being arrested. It was declined, so I applied again every year from then on.

The only way for me to get a passport was through my

brother again. He didn't have a Hungarian passport so he had acquired it by applying to the Hungarian Consulate in Canada, but in his application he used a photo of me instead of him. If anyone got suspicious, he had other ID to back up his identity; if I was using it, I had the benefit of looking more like the guy in the photo than my brother did. It was a win win! Although, one time my brother was on a train trying to enter Yugoslavia and the guy on the border checked his passport and refused to accept that the photo was him, but because other photographs with him looked like him, they had to accept it, but he got kicked off the train and had to wait 23 hours for the next one.

Me & Gyuszika in Santa Ana after a few & before a lots beers and joints

My first try using the passport was successful. My brother had a 10 year, unlimited entry visa to the United States so I went to visit Gyuszika and his sister Anikó in Santa Ana, California. Viki, you see I've been there, it's your turn now!

They told me that Güzü was coming from New York so it could be a great reunion. I spoke to Güzü too and we planned to go to New York together after visiting Gyuszika. There were some agencies hiring drivers to drive other people's cars from one city to another so we planned to find one from Los Angeles to New York. That way we could even earn money and see the States. I didn't want to use my return ticket, I wanted to buy a new one from New York to Toronto when I was ready to return. Unfortunately, on the airport the border patrol thought differently so I got a stamp in my passport stating that I had to leave the States on the date of my return flight, otherwise I'd be there illegally and lose my visa. I bought a cheap last-minute ticket and it was for two weeks only, so there wasn't enough time to visit New York.

I still had a great time but Americans are very different – I mean arseholes – compared to Canadians. Like at the border, where I always had a problem, in the shops, pubs, restaurants and generally everywhere I went and had to interact with them. Gyuszika was living in place where 8 or 10 houses had been built around a swimming pool. He rented the house with two Mexican friends from work. They were very friendly and didn't mind us crashing in the house. Actually, they supplied all the weed and coke and taught me how to drink 'shotgun'.

Once, we went to buy some booze and the girl at the cashier asked me for my ID. I didn't carry my passport but I had my driving licence with me. It was mine but with my brother's details and he was born on the 9th September, 1968. He was over 21 years old then. On the driving licence it was printed 09/09/1968 and the cashier asked me, which one is the day and which one is the month. I just simply asked her: 'Does it matter?' And she still stared at me waiting for an explanation, so I told her that if 'Either the first or the second is the month it would be still September, but even that doesn't matter because if you look at the year you should be able to calculate that I'm over 21 regardless of the month'. And that is why you kids have to study maths.

All the other customers behind me, including my friends, were laughing at her stupidity. You know what

157

she did? She refused to give me the booze because she said I was rude. So I told her that I wasn't being rude, I was being right and she was just angry because now everybody knew 'what a fucking idiot' she was. I asked her to call the manager but that didn't help either because after I explained everything to him, he still didn't give me my booze. I told them to 'fuck off' and asked Gyuszika to buy me the drink.

Gyuszika took us everywhere. We were sightseeing during the day and partying at night. We went to Long Beach, Hollywood to see the sign, the Chinese Theatre, the Walk of Fame with the stars, all the studios and he showed us lots of famous people's mansions too.

One night we went to a kind of remote area to see a garage band. The group actually played in a garage. There were rows of garages one after the other, so the crowd was between two rows. Everybody had to bring their own drink and drugs. The vibe was very similar to Hungarian concerts but the surroundings were very different. After a few hours the police showed up. They blocked both ends of the rows of garages and let people out one by one. There was a rubbish bin and if someone had any drink with them they had to throw it out before the police would let them go. So we sat in the car without any booze but drunk as hell and because I was from Canada, I became the driver. No one wanted to risk losing their driving licence, but if I had got caught, I could have got a new licence in Canada. I had never driven an automatic before so the guys gave me a quick lesson. The car was easy to drive, but when I had to slow down, I stepped on the brake as if it was a manual. It stopped so sudden that everybody from the back flew to the front. They forgot to mention the power brake.

After that everything was fine with the driving but we still had no alcohol. So the guys told me to go back. I parked the car nearby and because I was from Canada, I had to break the law again. I walked back and I didn't see anybody around the garages so I went to the bin quickly, grabbed as many bottles as I could and ran back to the car. Everybody was so happy. We went home and continued with the party.

The two weeks passed very quickly and then I had to return to Toronto and continue working in the pizza restaurant. It wasn't just work because it was summer, summer of 1990. Probably my best summer in Canada. I was single and free, kind of, because I still had to work. I took as much time off as I could. By then I had lots of friends but mostly Hungarians. We did many thing together and went to lots of places but the best was when we went camping.

Once, I think we took five cars and all of them were full. I was one of the drivers with my brother's Volkswagen Sirocco. My brother went back to Italy and Hungary that summer. That was the time when the Yugoslavian border guard noticed that my picture was in his passport and he had to spend a day at the station near the border before he could continue his journey to Hungary on the next train.

When we arrived at the campsite, a few of us went to the office to take care of our booking and the rest of us waited on the side road leading from the main road to the camp. Of course, we started drinking because we only were 10 metres from the camp's gate, so we thought it would be OK. Unfortunately, a police car was driving on the main road and spotted us drinking. Canada takes its drinking policies very strictly. You can't drink alcohol on public property and we weren't in the campsite yet. Although, we hid the open cans by the time the police could turn around and get to us, they still fined all the drivers $50, which we shared between the passengers.

After we got in and put up the tents, we resumed drinking, smoking weed and listening to music. That went on all night and the camp security came over several times before we all passed out. Of course, they kicked us out the next morning. They refunded our money but we didn't want to leave so they called the police – the same ones who had fined us the day before.

'Not you again,' said a tall stocky policeman with short ginger hair, when he recognised my face. 'What seems to be the problem?'

'Sir,' I said, trying to sound as calm and reasonable as possible, 'The camp men, they want us to leave now, which is OK, but I have been drinking and so you arrest me when I drive?'

'Have you drunk any alcohol this morning?' replied the cop.

'No, but too much yesterday. I do not want to break the law'.

'OK, here's what we'll do'.

He raised his voice and talked slowly: 'You drive away without making trouble and we won't arrest, we won't follow you, eh? We stay here for half an hour. You understand?' He pointed at his watch and then at the ground. 'We stay here. We will not follow you. We stay. Eh? You understand?'

That was all very well, but still there was no way that I was going to drive away from the campsite while they were still there. I shook my head and walked away. This wasn't good for us if we couldn't find a solution. Finally, one of the campers, who had partied with us the previous evening, helped me out. Using his own car, he gently shunted my car out of the camp, without me having to start the engine. As soon as I was outside, I fired up the engine and quickly drove away.

We probably drove for an hour until the guys in the first car spotted a small side road leading into the forest. We drove along it until we came to a house. We knocked on the door, because we wanted to ask their permission to camp on their land but no one was home. We put up our tents and continued with the booze, drugs and music. A few hours later, the police showed up. I don't know what they were doing there, but they found us. These were different police than the ones from the camp.

Luckily, there was a Canadian-Hungarian guy with us who had read the names on the envelopes in the mailbox when we had visited the house. His perfect English and knowledge about the owners was enough for the police to believe our story that we were camping with the owners' permission. So they left us alone.

Zsolti laughing at us after disappearing from the forest

We got drunk and stoned and we even took some mushrooms. We found a small lake not far from us and went for a swim too. Happy times. We stayed up all night and at dawn we noticed that one of us was missing. The guy's name was Zsolti and his wife Csilla realised that she hadn't seen him for a while. Everybody started to look for him. After a few hours, we decided to drive into the nearby town and ask for help. The last time someone had seen him was by the lake, so we were afraid he had drowned. The police arrived very quickly and lots of people from the town came to help find him. Some people came on quad bikes, others on foot. I'm not sure if there was a diver in the lake, but I know that a police helicopter was involved. Csilla called home to Toronto many times from the town but there was no answer, so the search continued.

It was about 6:00pm when finally he answered his wife's call in Toronto. Csilla told us and everybody else who helped with the search that Zsolti in his drunkenness had decided to hitchhike home to Toronto. Someone had picked him up, but because it was too late they spent a night in a camp. Zsolti partied with them all night and the next day they took him to Toronto. We had no mobile phones then so it wasn't so easy to call someone, like it is today.

When Zsolti got home, he fell asleep and only woke up when the phone rang around 6:00pm. Everybody was so pleased that nothing bad had happened to him that nobody said a bad word or was angry even though it was his fault that he hadn't told anyone, not even his wife, that he was leaving. It was so touching to see how readily the whole town, with the police and a helicopter helped us, even when they saw how fucked up we were. OK, kids, sometimes you can trust the police.

CHAPTER EIGHTEEN

LIFE'S A GAS

I suffered the pizza job in Canada for about a year but Europe beckoned again. It was too much to resist, especially since Tigi, told me about a new scam that you could do with credit cards. Nothing was done electrically then; everyone used those manual credit card imprinter machines which made an impression of the embossed card details on carbon paper slips. That was so easy to scam because all you had to do was fake the signature.

So I jumped on a plane to Amsterdam with Miki. Even this time, I travelled with my brother's passport again, which had my photograph in it.

We didn't want to stay in Amsterdam; we just wanted to look around quickly and visit some of those famous coffee shops. We stayed there for a couple of days getting drunk, stoned and high while my big tall angry friend Péter, who was still in Germany, negotiated the sale of the car there. We hitchhiked from there to Germany and got picked up by a lorry driver. The border checks for lorry drivers was different from what I had seen before. All he had to do was go into the passport check building, then got back into the lorry and drove us over the border, so we never got checked, even though on this occasion I actually had a valid passport, albeit my brother's.

Whilst he was driving, the lorry driver was popping amphetamines and smoking weed and he even shared some with us too, so it would have been churlish of us to think ill of him for risking all our young lives by being drugged off his tits. Actually, that turned out to be the best hitchhike of my life. After a very pleasant journey, he dropped us off at Stuttgart and from there we went to meet Péter in Tübingen and get the car. It was a small car. I can't remember what it was. I do remember we only paid him DM500 for it so it must have been a proper shit heap.

Having fun with the police in Körmend with my brother's passport in my back pocket

I did actually go back to Hungary, posing as my brother, but I could only go to a part of the country where nobody knew me – a place in the far west called Körmend, just over the border from Austria where Miki was from.

Miki was supporting me financially but I promised him as soon as we got to Vienna and did some credit card scams, I would pay him back and that's what I did. I also had four or five credit cards I had borrowed from friends, which they had then cancelled. This didn't stop me from using them though, because shops rarely phoned the credit companies to check if the cards were active. The trouble was, there weren't many places in Hungary at that time that would accept credit cards, but I used them where I could.

We picked up two young girls in Hungary, and then

popped over to Split, a coastal town in Yugoslavia, with them for a week's mini break. This was August 1990. Then we went back to Hungary and drove around various places. Under cover of night, I even drove to Szeged, picked up my parents and took them to Siófok on the southern bank of Lake Balaton, the most famous and biggest lake in Hungary. We stayed there for about four days, but no one knew me there, so I could relax.

I remembered the last time when I was in Siófok with my friends, Rubber, Imi, Szkuri, Gyuszika and his sister Aniko, who was Imi's girlfriend at the time. It was the summer of 1985, I think. We hardly had any money so we hitchhiked there in pairs. Rubber was with me because he was my best friend then, Imi was with Anikó of course and Szkuri was with Gyuszika. I don't know how we did it, but Rubber and I arrived at Siófok first. By the time the others arrived, we had already spent all our money on booze. We didn't have enough money for accommodation so we spent the nights under the sky on the shore of Balaton. The others had some money but not much, so we couldn't eat or drink in a pub or restaurant. We usually bought some bread and salami or jam and stole pure alcohol (96% alcohol) and fruit syrup. We mixed together some pure alcohol, water and fruit syrup in a two-litre plastic bottle and we drank that. To other people it looked like some kind of fruit squash so they were wondering how we got so pissed from it.

Sometimes we went to a food kiosk on the beach and waited until someone left some food on their plate and we just sat down and ate it. It was mostly fish and chips. Unfortunately, after five days Imi got caught stealing from a store so it was the end of his holiday. We stayed for a few more days but by then the police were waking us up almost every morning. They were fed up with us and threatened us with a few nights in a lock up, so it was in everybody's best interests to return to Szeged.

Anyway, let's get back to 1990. Politically, the entire country had changed by then, so there was little incentive for people to turn me in anyway, but I still wanted to be careful as I hadn't received an official pardon. The country certainly felt different. When we used to party before, the police would be all over the place, they would routinely arrest us and beat us up. When I went to Budapest, I visited one of the most infamous clubs which was called The Black Hole, where people were openly taking drugs, snorting coke from the table in plain view. There is no way that could have happened previously, they would instantly have been arrested, because there were spies everywhere.

If I were to go back now, in 2022, nobody would be sniffing coke off the table. That brief period of anything goes, was typical during a time of transition. Now, things have settled down so law and order had found its proper level.

The older people all looked the same – just as miserable as ever. They weren't making good money, always behind with payments, all complaining how much better it was before, under communism, when everyone had a job and got paid. But even the Hungarian government knew it couldn't sustain a policy of full employment, so things had to change.

Some people got very rich quickly under the new regime, for sure. And what did these people wear to show that they were doing very well? What else, but the universal signifiers of new money with no taste? Bling. Lots of gold jewellery. Those people were poor for a long time, so when they got money they wanted to demonstrate to everyone else, so the inevitable bling came to the fore.

After a nice holiday on Siófok with my parents, I went back to Körmend with my girlfriend and spent a few nights there until someone took me to Vienna. I still had credit cards so I stayed there for about two weeks and made the most of the 'plastic'. When I only had one card left, I went to Tübingen, Germany to say goodbye to Péter and of course, we went to Überlingen as well because I couldn't leave before I said goodbye to my best friend Tigi.

CHAPTER NINETEEN

HERE TODAY, GONE TOMORROW

After my visit to Hungary and two months spent in Europe, I flew back from Amsterdam to Toronto in September 1990 to celebrate my brother's birthday again. And of course, I went back to work to Pizza Pizza.

Two months later I visited the States again but now with my friend Miki, to celebrate the birthday of an old friend from Szeged. I used my brother's passport again. But we ran into problems at the Niagara Falls and Buffalo border. The border guards took the car apart, looking for contraband. The guard told us right up front that he wasn't going to let us through, he just needed to find a good reason to turn us back. My brother had a conviction for marijuana possession, which didn't help. Anyway, eventually they found it out and we were turned away.

We had to try a different border to cross so we drove to Montreal and instead of trying to cross legally with my passport, I crossed the border the same way as I used to do in Europe. So Miki had to drive through on his own, with his clean passport and I crossed the border illegally on foot and met up with him on the other side. We were in a hurry because we hasn't factored on a failed border crossing in our journey time so Miki drove fast along the icy roads and so inevitably we ended up in the ditch. Miki went for help I was left with the car. The snow was so deep in the ditch that we couldn't open the doors so Miki opened the window and dug himself through the snow from there. Only the headlights were visible. Miki got back in a few hours but by then I was wearing all my clothes it was so cold. I thought I was going to freeze to death. So we were rescued and the car was towed out of the ditch. We could have driven anywhere, but we stayed in the States – in Burlington, Vermont – for about two weeks. I have been told that even most Americans have never been to Vermont, but that's where my refugee friend had been placed after registering as a refugee in Austria, so that's where we had to go to visit him. Vermont was a very opulent place.

This friend of mine in Burlington even used to be our driver in Vienna when we had no car. His wife was an interesting case. My friend drank a lot and passed out many times; whenever he did that, his wife went to a club by herself. Or if someone was around and spent the night with them, she would make sweet love with the guest. That is why I liked to spent lots of nights with them in Vienna. Now that was hospitality! I was hoping that the same thing would happen to me in Burlington too. Let's just say, I wasn't disappointed.

The shops practically invited shoplifting – everything was on display close to the exit! But we didn't want to get into that because we had just arrived, we didn't know anything about the stores, we had no background. In Europe it was different because we knew seasoned shoplifters who could give us advice about which shops to hit and which to avoid. But here in Vermont we were blind. But once we went shopping with my friend, we could see how easy it was to shoplift, so we used the same old distraction technique to steal a few camcorders, cameras, CD players. Miki was an honest guy and we didn't want to ruin his vacation, so we only did a few shops and then we stopped. The rest of the vacation was spent drinking and having fun and for me having sex, then we returned to Canada after two weeks.

We all hid our stolen items in the car but thanks to my luck, they searched us at the border and found everything. Luckily, they thought we had bought them and that we just wanted to avoid paying the duty. Since it was our first time, they just made us pay the duty but they warned us that the next time they would impound our car as well as any items we attempted to smuggle.

When we got back to Canada, I decided that I needed more reliable identification than my brother's old driving licence. It was OK to use for age verification in a bar, but if I'd been stopped by the police while driving, a quick check would have shown that it was invalid. So I need something better. Fortunately, my brother still had his refugee passport which had been issued in Italy so that he could travel to Canada. He didn't need it anymore because that passport was only good for a one way trip from Italy to Canada but it was still usable for identification. So I removed the old photo and replaced it with my own, changed the name and date of birth to my own. It was very easy to do that in those days. Even the blue rubber stamp was easy to fake. Then I went to the Ministry of Transportation and used my brother's old doctored passport for identification. I couldn't read English very well but I had to do a multiple choice test. Luckily, a friend of mine who had already taken the test, told me the answers and all I had to do was memorise them.

I passed the multiple choice test with full marks and I was given a provisional genuine Canadian driving license in December 1990. Then my brother taught me how to drive, in his small Honda Civic. I took my driving test and passed.

CHAPTER TWENTY

POISON HEART

By January 1991 I was bored again, working in Pizza Pizza for shitty money, so I borrowed my brother's passport again and went back to Vienna to visit old friends. So it was back to couch-hopping at the houses of various friends until I found somewhere more permanent to live at a friend of a friend's house. When I arrived there, his ex-wife was about to move out the following week – her bags were already packed. But we formed an instant attraction, so we started a relationship under the same roof. Then we moved out together. She later became my first real wife. My first marriage didn't count because there was no love, it was for me to be able to stay in Canada. Unfortunately, my first real wife got tired of me and kicked me out years and years later, so she became my ex-wife, but at this point in my story none of this had happened yet, but still, from now on in my book I'll call her my future ex-wife until she became my ex-wife.

So my future ex-wife rented a small one-bedroom flat. She and I slept in the bedroom and seven of our friends slept scattered around the small flat, on the floor or couch. My future ex-wife was working in a store called Prenatal which sold maternity clothes. She was the only one of us with a job. We lived there for almost a year, then I took my future ex-wife back to Canada in December 1991.

Let me tell you kids about our typical day: my future

ex-wife woke up and went to work, then the rest of us would eventually stir, wash and dress, maybe open a few cans of lager left over from the previous night. Waiting for eight people to use the bathroom takes a little time, but we weren't in any hurry. Someone would make breakfast.

Balázs, Árpi, me & Imi cooking dinner and getting pissed in the flat

Only two of us were smokers, so they'd go outside (most of the time) to do that. By the time we were all ready, it was probably about midday, so we'd hit the town to do a little bit of shoplifting. Not much though. If we stole one pair of jeans and sold it on, that would give enough money to all of us to live, eat and drink all day. We all pooled the money we made from shoplifting.

We all made sure to dress smartly so that we didn't arouse suspicion in the shops that we targeted. We tended to avoid the main shopping areas in Vienna because there were lots of police dressed as civilians around there. They didn't want rich tourists to be robbed, so that's where the police placed most of their resources.

We stole in small groups and rotated the stores, so we wouldn't hit the same place two days in a row. Sometimes, one of us might sit out for a day, because he felt unlucky, or had a hunch that he might get caught. We always targeted items that we could sell on easily – jeans, T-shirts, sweat shirts, trainers, Walkmans, camcorders, cameras, CDs and CD players. We stole to order. We couldn't always steal what we wanted and had to settle for whatever we could get away with. Sometimes we even stole large objects such as a VCR from the window display, so long as one of us was able to distract the shop owner and get him to turn the other way. As you can see kids, it was just like before or even better and easier.

We also knew an Austrian guy who ran a shop selling classical music CDs and he would give us lists of CDs to steal from other shops (usually the megastores) – his competitors – and he would buy them from us for half price and then put them directly on the shelves of his store. Typically a pair of us could steal 60 CDs per day. The multipacks and box sets were the best, because they slipped easily under a jacket and they were more expensive than a single CD.

One day Imi was my partner in crime and we went to hit a big CD store on Kärtner Straße. It was a very risky business to steal on the main shopping street of Vienna but we felt lucky that day. We knew that they put alarm strips on the CDs so that was no surprise. I was the one cutting the strips out and Imi was the one stealing them. I think I put 4 or 5 box sets together in one place, hidden from the sales staff. Imi went there and put them under his jacket. Everything seemed great. Imi went out first and I was right behind him, when the alarm started to ring. Imi started running along Kärtner Straße where there were lots of civilian clothed police, so he didn't know if he was running towards one. Like I said, risky business. The salesmen wanted to run after him but I blocked the door and acted like the alarm came on because of me. I didn't move from the door and told them that I had nothing on me, which was true, and I tried to hamper them as much as possible. They knew that Imi was the thief not me and they tried to push me away but by the time they got through me, Imi was so far away they couldn't catch him. We always had a meeting place if something like this happened, so I went there and Imi was waiting for me.

We took the box sets apart to see what had happened. The stores had got smarter after noticing that lots of CDs were missing, so they had put an extra alarm strip inside the box set too. We went to sell the CDs, then took the rest of the day off and went drinking.

Imi, me & Tigi after the 'action' and before the drinking

Sometimes we'd stop in smaller villages to see what we could shoplift, and sometimes we got lucky. Bigger cities were better. Sometimes, it was absurd how brazen we were. Occasionally, when we were stealing to order, we would be given instructions to steal a specific item maybe at the back of the store, which made it harder. Tigi was definitely the most brazen of us all. One time he simply walked into a shop and then strode confidently outside with a VCR under his arm, without even attempting to hide it.

Another time, Tigi stole a VCR to order from right at the back of a store, by hiding it on his back, underneath his coat. This meant that he still had space at the front of his coat to steal something else. He couldn't resist. So I think he stuck a camcorder in the front of his coat, but then he looked so misshapen it would have been obvious what he was doing to anyone who looked at him, so we had to walk out, three of us together in a line, with Tigi sandwiched in the middle of us. That was so risky, but we got away with it. I suppose it was so outrageous that we didn't immediately fall under suspicion.

The well deserved reward after a hard day's work with Tigi

We made our best money stealing bikes in Vienna and then selling them to a guy we knew who ran a bike shop in Budapest. Tigi, Imi and I stole six bikes between us, two each, and then we took a train with our girlfriends and a bike each to the border, got off just before the border, and rode across the border on the bikes. On the Hungarian side of the border we caught the train to Budapest where we gave them to our friend, who could sell them in full confidence that they would never be traced because they had been stolen from another country. We each got paid 60,000 Hungarian forints, which was about ten times what my parents earned in a month. We made other trips to Hungary with smaller items such as cameras and camcorders. At one time my net worth was about 100,000 Hungarian forints which was 16 months salary for my parents.

After selling the bikes, we spent a few days living it up

in Hungary and we spent a lots of money there. Tigi was a very heavy gambler, so he lost all of his money playing slot machines and video poker in less than a week. When we picked him up, he was broke.

One time I went to Kecskemét – a city halfway between Budapest and Szeged – because my friend, Csaszi was living there. He was broke. I told him that he could make good money stealing bicycles, but he didn't want to do that anymore. He wanted to stay in Hungary. But he did have a scam that he wanted to perform but he needed me, so I helped him out. First he got me a fake Hungarian ID, I rented a video camera and then we sold it to someone that Csaszi already had lined up. The proprietor of the rentals place took some video footage of me, as security in case I didn't bring back the video camera. This didn't worry me because as soon as we had sold it, we drove about 200km away to Balaton.

After spending a week in Balaton, having a great holiday with the money we had earned from selling the video camera, I phoned my future ex-wife in Vienna and told her everything was fine. Moments later, the police arrived and arrested me. It turned out that the wife of the guy I had stolen the camera from, just happened to have gone on holiday in the exact same place. Balaton is a huge resort. She could have gone anywhere in that area, but she happened to be waiting in the very queue for the same pay phone while I was speaking to my future ex-wife and she recognised me from the video footage her husband had taken. The odds of her being there must have been over a million to one.

The police arrested me, I spent the night in the cell and then they transferred me to Kecskemét for a line up. The husband and wife correctly identified me and of course, the video evidence was irrefutable. The crazy thing was, I didn't even need to do that scam. I had plenty of money and just did it for a favour for Csaszi. Csaszi was useless.

Do you remember kids, I told you when he wanted to rob that poor guy in the hospital in Italy who broke both his arms and a leg, that I should have known how much of a fucking arsehole Csaszi is and I shouldn't have trusted him? This was the reason. He disappeared, although I don't know how much he could have done. Apparently, he was convinced that I was going to give him up, which I didn't do. It would have been very foolish for me to do that anyway, because he knew that I was on a false passport. If he had revealed my true identity, I could have been imprisoned in Hungary for ten years for my AWOL conviction. I would far rather go to jail for a few months for stealing a video camera than have my real identity revealed. The third guy – the guy who got me the false Hungarian ID – was actually very helpful. He even arranged a lawyer for me.

The lawyer said it would be best for me if I implicated someone, because they knew that I couldn't get a false ID on my own. So the third guy agreed to take the rap for that, which was very generous of him. I spent about ten days in jail, then I was bailed pending a hearing two months' later. I had to stay in Kecskemét until my sentence date, when I received one year in prison, suspended for two years. I should have gone to jail for that crime, but my lawyer managed to bribe the judge because they had been to school together. The bribe cost me a small fortune – when I add everything together, lawyer, trial cost, the cost of the video camera, my future ex-wife's travel expenses and missed work, the bribe and everything else it came to half a million Hungarian forint. It not only cleared me out, but took all my future ex-wife's savings as well. So all the money I had saved up from stealing over a period of several months, ended up in the pocket of a corrupt judge. It was the first time in my life that I had a bank account, which was now completely empty. Everything was looking great and then I was cleared out of all my money.

Finally I was in Vienna again, back in the flat with my friends.

Szkuri, me, Imi & Rubber, the next morning after celebrating my arrival

We continued stealing from stores and I tried to put some money together again. We heard about a very good deal from the others: stealing art. The others told us what kind of art we should steal and where to sell it. Those pictures were copperplate printings but who cared, they told us that we'd get good money for them.

We stole about five and went to sell them. Because we never sold anything to that store we were careful. We sent my future ex-wife into the store with one picture only. The owner liked it and paid good money for it and told her that if she had more she should bring it over the next day and by then he would have more money to pay for them. So that's what we did.

The next day she took the pictures to the store to sell them. We were waiting for her closed by. After about 15 minutes I got suspicious and I went to the store to see what was happening. When I got to the store a guy was standing at the door and only opened it a little bit to tell me that they were closed. I knew right away what was happening so I kicked the door in and because I always carried pepper spray, started to spray him and the next guy and the next one.

I fought my way to the back of the store, where two guys were holding my future ex-wife, and I tried to free her. The two fat guys just jumped on her, buried her under their sweaty morbidly obese carcasses like a couple of town hall Saturday night wrestlers. They were so heavy I couldn't free her. The other guy had got to me by then so I was spraying, kicking and hitting about five guys but I couldn't rescue my future ex-wife from under the mountain of perspiring adipose tissue. I knew the police had been called and I didn't have much time so I told her that I had to leave because if I had been arrested after what I did, I would never have breathed the sweet air of freedom ever again.

As I fought my way out of the shop and I shouted to her: 'Tell the police: some Hungarians paid you to sell the pictures. That's all. You didn't know they were stolen. If they want names, make one up'.

The police let her go a few hours later and I think she only got a warning because it looked like she had used bad judgment, by agreeing to sell this art work for some Hungarian men, and she was able to convince them that she didn't realise that she was fencing stolen goods and that she certainly hadn't stolen them herself.

When we all met up we asked her what had happened. She told us that we stole the pictures from the store owner's brother and he recognised them, and that's how he knew they were stolen. She confessed that she had given the police my real name. 'What the fuck?' I said, 'Why? You could've told them any name, it would have made no difference to them'.

I should have known then not to trust her anymore but

I was in love so I was stupid, but that bit me in the arse later.

An article about my attack appeared in the local paper, which I kept for many years. When my future ex-wife kicked me out, she kept this article along with many more of my belongings, like my precious pictures and negatives from my journeys through my life that I never could replace, just to piss me off. She's probably thrown them out by now but she wouldn't give it to me because that would have made me happy.

Now I was a wanted man again and my name was in the paper. I didn't want any more bad luck in Europe. But at least I was a free man, so my future ex-wife and I decided to head for Canada. Now that the trial was over in Hungary, I was free to travel again. I couldn't do any more crime in Hungary, because the moment I broke the terms of my parole, I would be sent to prison.

I was in love with my future ex-wife and she was in love with me, so when I asked her to come with me to Canada, she agreed.

CHAPTER TWENTY-ONE

I DON'T WANT TO GROW UP

So we left Austria on 15th December 1991 and arrived in Canada the next day. I was still travelling on my brother's Hungarian passport. The regime in Hungary was less repressive by now so I could no longer seek refugee asylum status. I could only stay if I got married, so my brother and I agreed to marry each other's girlfriends. We did it soon after we got there in February 1992.

My brother's girlfriend was Canadian, so I secured my place in the country by marrying her. My brother was by now a Canadian citizen himself, so marrying my future-ex wife meant that she too could stay in the country. We didn't make a big deal out of it; we just had to invite a few friends and took some pictures to make the weddings look authentic.

My brother's story with my future ex-wife was believable because they were both Hungarians. He said that he had met my future ex-wife while he was in Hungary just about two years before, but even after he went back to Canada they stayed in touch and she eventually agreed to come to live with him in Canada.

My story was different. I knew that immigration must have been highly suspicious of me, getting married after being in Canada for only two months. I still spoke barely any English and my 'wife' spoke no Hungarian. Then there was the small matter of living together. Fortunately, my brother had a two-bedroom flat in Mississauga, West of Toronto, at 2339 Park Towers Avenue, so we all moved in there together.

I still had to use an alias to get married. I couldn't get married on my own name because as we found out there was an agreement between Hungary and Canada to extradite escaped soldiers so I became Lacika, my best friend from Hungary.

When my brother got married to my future ex-wife, everything went without a hitch. That's possibly why I became a little careless at my own wedding. I thought nothing bad could happen but unfortunately, a little mistake slipped into the proceedings. Thankfully, it was correctable.

I was so unfocused during the marriage ceremony that when the marriage celebrant asked my mother's name, I forgot that I wasn't using my own name to get married, I was using Lacika's. So I blurted out my own mother's name instead of his. Fortunately, just a few minutes later after the marriage celebrant had left the room, it occurred to me that I had fucked up. There was an immediate panic in the room. My mind was spinning. How could I fix this? Who the hell messes up their own mother's name? How many mothers must you have to give the wrong answer to that simple question? The only thing I knew for sure was that my real mother's name couldn't stay on my marriage certificate. I was thinking very hard how could I correct this mistake without being suspected of lying.

Two minutes later, when the marriage celebrant returned, I was ready with my explanation. I wonder kids, what would you have figured out in two minutes, to explain why you got your own mother's name wrong? Luckily, I was very good at lying. I told the marriage celebrant that I was a child of foster parents and I had automatically given the name of my foster mother, even though I should have said the name of my birth mother, with whom I had had no relationship during my whole life. Fortunately, I presented the lie so convincingly that the marriage celebrant didn't suspect anything; he agreed to correct my mother's name and my wedding continued smoothly. That is how my brother's girlfriend became my first wife, but as I mentioned earlier, I don't count this as a real marriage as it was just so I could stay in Canada. Unfortunately, to this day, I am not a citizen of Canada.

My future ex-wife was pregnant so I decided that it was time for me to leave my life of casual crime behind, settle down and get a proper honest job with a future. My friend, Miki was making good money working as a carpet fitter for a large company. They worked in a two-man crew. One was the boss, who drove the van and had the tools and the other person was the helper. But in my case, I became an apprentice for a Maltese guy called Carmel and only later became a helper because I didn't know how to fit carpet first; Miki set me up with him. He had to teach me how to install carpets, but it was easy, I picked it up quickly but then I was young and fit, so the physical side wasn't a problem.

The other good thing about that job was that when in 1994 Woolko stores were sold to rival Walmart, they hired our company to install carpet in every stores in Canada. So I have been everywhere from Newfoundland to British Columbia. They flew us everywhere, they paid for the hotel and for a rental car and we got a company credit card as well.

Our company was in the union so even the time they gave us to do the work was plenty. We had to work at night after the store closed at 10:00pm and we always finished the daily allowed area in 4–5 hours so we had enough time to sleep and go sightseeing the next day before work. For the smaller stores we got 2 weeks to finish but we finished them in 6–7 days, and for the bigger stores we got 3 weeks but we finished them in 2 weeks so we had lots of time after that to look around, go sightseeing and everything was paid for.

Of course, we couldn't work on weekends so that was free for us to do whatever we wanted to. If we wanted we could come home after finishing a store but who is stupid enough to ruin a free vacation, so we stayed, except one time when my brother's son Tommy was born.

And if we are already talking about birth, on the 5th October 1992 you were born Krisztina. That was the best day of my life up to that point. But because my brother was still married to your mother, he had to appear on all official paperwork (like your birth certificate) as your father because we were still waiting for your mother's citizenship. But I returned the favour, when my brother's girlfriend, my 'wife' gave birth to Tommy, I become his father on all the documents.

We moved out of my brother's flat soon after you were born Krisztina. Things got too crowded and my brother was/is very easy to quarrel with. He would pick on everyone if things were not the way he wanted them. Even today he will get into physical fights. My brother and I had a few heated arguments, so it was time to move on.

Me, Tigi & my brother in Canada before my future ex-wife kicked Tigi out

Our first flat was in the South-west side of Toronto at

1621 Queen Street West, which was a very shitty, low rent area at that time. During the day it was kind of OK, but at night the sex workers and drug dealers ruled the street. It wasn't the place for families, so after six months we moved to a more family-friendly area and we rented a flat at 45 Grenoble Drive on the North-east side of Toronto. Even Tigi came to visit me there but of course, my future ex-wife didn't like it so after two nights he had to move to my brother's flat.

By then I had set up on my own and had become self-employed. I went to work freelance for a smaller shop, and that's when I started to make good money, about $10,000 per month. I had to spend about half of that on paying a helper and buying materials, but I was still clearing $5,000 profit each month. Other Hungarians I knew were working in places like Pizza Pizza which was very poorly paid. I was making about four times more than them, so I felt good.

In the beginning of 1995, my future ex-wife received her Canadian citizenship, so she and my brother were able to get divorced. I had to wait another three years for my citizenship, after which I divorced my brother's girlfriend. But remember kids, I received the citizenship under Lacika's name. So the plan was that, when I received an amnesty from Hungary, so that I wouldn't get extradited, then I could get a Hungarian passport under my own name, marry my future ex-wife and get the Canadian citizenship under my own name. Of course, things didn't actually work out that way but I think you kids know that.

And then you came, Attila, on 8th September, 1995 and that was the second best day of my life and this time I was the official father. So now I had you, Attila, and I was your official father under my real name, you Krisztina, with my brother as the official father and my brother had Tommy with me as the official father but under Lacika's name.

My father, me & my mother in Canada

Unfortunately, my mother was diagnosed with lung cancer so we brought her and my father to Canada so they can meet you, Krisztina and Attila.

Business still seemed to be booming at that time, and there was a lots of demand for carpet fitters. So even though it was manual labour, it was very lucrative and in 1996 I was able to take out a mortgage of $95,000 on a 120m^2 flat in a condo just outside Toronto and North of Mississauga in a suburb called Brampton at 30 Malta Avenue, which was a huge step up for us. It only cost about $1,400 a month. There was 24 -hour security, a swimming pool, tennis court, gym, sauna and my rent also covered the heating and the air-conditioning in the summer, water, cleaning, almost everything.

There was nothing much of interest to report, then. I was just working diligently in the carpet shop. I went to concerts and festivals with friends because my future ex-wife lost interest in almost everything. She hardly came with me anywhere, although, she was invited just like me. If it was a party at a friend's place who had kids too, then I took you, Krisztina, and even you, Attila, when you got old enough. Of course, I went without your mother to concerts and festivals too because she didn't want to come with me. I saw lots of my favourite bands there. As I mentioned earlier kids, I saw The Ramones 3–4 times and I also went to see Bad Manners, The Specials, The Beat, The Selecter and many other groups, but what I didn't mention was that I saw them in Canada.

Once, we went to a festival about two hours' drive from Toronto. We went there with two cars and I drove my van with four friends onboard. But before we left we stopped at an LCBO to buy vodka and at Burger King to buy some soft drinks. We drank some of the soft drink and filled the cup up with vodka. So for someone outside the van it looked like we were drinking a soft drink from Burger King and this way we avoided others on the road calling the police on us. It worked fine until we actually got to the town where the festival was being held. The police were waiting for us and waved us off to the side of the road.

When I asked 'What's wrong?' they told me that someone had called to report that we had been acting suspiciously in the van. What a fucking arsehole! But Canadians are like that. If something is not right, they call the police right away.

The police's first move was to stick a stupid breathalyser in my mouth and when I blew into it I was just over the limit so the police could only suspend my driving licence for 24 hours. The other two cars with us also stopped and one of our friends who was sober drove my van to the festival. We got in without any difficulties and started drinking and seeing groups right away.

I always had my backpack on because I had become used to it in Europe when we were stealing or crossing borders. I had my 'survival kit' in it. I still take my backpack with me everywhere even today. Anyway, we went from one group to the next and drank more and more. I always liked to be at the front of concerts and this festival was no different. I got separated from my friends but it wasn't a problem because we always had a spot where we met from time to time or waited for the others to show up.

At this festival I performed my first and last stage diving. I climbed up on the stage and dived into the crowd backwards. Luckily, the crowd caught me and then sent me back to the edge of the crowd passing me from hand to hand. It was amazing! I only noticed later, when we wanted to go to sleep in my van, that my backpack was open and I had lost everything from it, including the key for my van. Because I was the only one with backpack, my friends had put all kinds of stuff in it, like CDs and T-shirts they had bought at the festival and I lost everything. We tried to find the key, at least, but we had no such luck.

The next day, when we were ready to go home, five of us who had come in my van had to squeeze in to the other two cars. It was a very uncomfortable two-hour drive back to Toronto. Besides not having any room in the car to stretch our legs, everybody had a massive hangover. Luckily, I had a spare key at home but it still meant that my future ex-wife and I had to drive back to the town where the festival was held, go to the police station to pick up my driving licence and then get my van and drive back home. It took us about six hours but my van and I eventually got safely home.

I even used to grow weed with my brother at one time. They were hydroponics and my brother was very good at growing them as he had done it before. Unfortunately, at first he teamed up with a wrong guy. We knew him from Hungary but he was always a loser so we never were friends. I'm not sure what my brother saw in him in Canada but it was a big mistake.

My brother had been growing weed for a while in his bedroom when he became friends with this loser. This guy couldn't hold down a job and saw good money in the weed business so he asked my brother to help him out.

The plan was to split the money in half. So my brother set this guy's bedroom up with his own money and all this idiot had to do was maintain the operation. How hard could that be? He was living there. But he still managed to screw it up.

His name was Csaba Sipter and everybody should avoid him. I think the water pump broke down but he didn't go in the bedroom to check on the plants, so they dried out and died. My brother invested lots of money in it for no return. But imagine this kids: when my brother's plants were ready and he sold them, this loser wanted half of that money. My brother told him straight: 'In my flat is my operation and my money only; in your flat is our operation and our money. You fucked up our operation so you have no money. It's as simple as that.' So guess what this little shit did after my brother helped him out? He called the police on him. What a rat! My brother's only luck was that the police didn't have a search warrant so his case was thrown out of court but they still seized all his equipment. After this, he was afraid to start again in his flat so he teamed up with me. I rented a one-bedroom flat and we bought new equipment. We set up the room together and my brother taught me how to grow hydroponics so I went to the flat every day after work to check on the plants and to do the daily maintenance. My brother came up probably once a week to see how everything was going. Everything was fine. I only asked one thing from my brother and that was to tell no one, not even his wife.

I rented the flat so it was my risk and my brother didn't risk anything. Of course, he didn't comply and told his wife everything about our operation. Their relationship was in a ditch so I was afraid that if they broke up, his wife would call the police just to hurt my brother, without realising that she would only be hurting me.

The first 'harvest' took the longest because we didn't

have cuttings, but we still made good money. The second 'harvest' could have been quicker because we used cuttings but unfortunately, my brother's wife left my brother in a very ugly separation, so we had to close down our operation. We wouldn't have had any problem if my brother had just listened and had kept everything secret, especially from his wife.

Lacika received the Canadian citizenship in 1998 so I divorced my brother's girlfriend and my future ex-wife and I got married on 4th June under my original name. That marriage didn't last very long. My brother also married his girlfriend, and had another child, Jacklin.

CHAPTER TWENTY-TWO

TEENAGE LOBOTOMY

Kids, the next few pages aren't going to be about an hilarious era of my life, but about what has greatly influenced it, to this day.

This section is mainly for you, Krisztina and Attila, as I will now describe how and why our relationship was ruined by your mother. It would have been more appropriate for me to tell you this personally, but since your mother banned us from contacting each other, I had no choice but to write it down.

Our relationship with your mother, especially the sexual part of it, had already deteriorated since you were born Krisztina, but it was still bearable. But after your birth, Attila, our sex life dropped to almost zero. Regardless of that, even after you arrived Attila, we went to house parties with the other families with kids for quite some time, but for the last two years I almost always went to every party with you guys or alone because your mother didn't feel like coming.

I was working a lot at the time because we had won a contract with the Toronto District School Board to replace the old floor coverings, which of course had to be done after our day-to-day work and after the kids went home from the schools. I started at 9:00am and got home around 2:00–3:00am the following morning. I was still young then so it was OK. There were also times when I didn't have a day off for three months. It's true that I earned well because as I mentioned earlier, I took home $5,000 a month. Your mother was at home with you guys and did not work. Anyway, when I got home at dawn, no matter how tired I was, I still had the strength for sex. Unfortunately, not your mother. Sadly, she got so tired being at home all the time, that there was a period that we had no sex for six weeks. I wasn't even thirty then. Even now, aged over fifty, I have more sex with Anita. Back then, I had sex with your mother once in six weeks, while now with Anita I have sex six times a week. It's close but not the same.

I talked about this with your mother, Krisztina and Attila, many times and also told her that I wasn't going to look for sex with anyone else, but that if someone tried to seduce me, I might not be able to say no. Still, nothing changed in the bedroom, at least not on my part, but now that I think back, she may have had an affair with someone else then, not just towards the end of our relationship, and she was only withholding sex from me. Maybe her other sex life was perfectly healthy.

I once went to play billiards with my brother and his wife. I knew they liked threesomes and the subject came up while we were drinking; they invited me to join them if I felt like it. Then came the moment I was afraid of. I was drunk but mostly horny, so I couldn't say no. I had the opportunity to do it again a couple of weeks later, but after the first time I had such a guilty conscience that since we were drunk again, I pretended I had passed out.

It took maybe a month to digest the knowledge that I had cheated on your mother kids, but after that I couldn't take it any longer and confessed to what I had done. I had warned her that if there was no sex at home, then sooner or later this could happen. I honestly told her everything and we agreed to stay together for the time being, and that if she couldn't forgive me later on, we would divorce.

I didn't cheat on your mother, Krisztina and Attila, before or since that one time and I think I was reasonable even in the cheating because I confessed voluntarily; I didn't leave her to find out from someone else. Also, it only happened because there was no sex at home.

Your mother told me that if we divorced, she didn't want to be with anyone for a while because she had had enough of guys because of me. Nevertheless, she cheated on me even before our separation. More specifically, she had an affair that lasted beyond our separation. I only suspected that she had cheated on me once when I first caught her lying to me, but unfortunately, that wasn't the case. After the first one, more and more lies came.

The first time I caught her lying was when she went to play billiards with her 'girlfriends'. At that time in Canada, everything shut down at 2:00am. She still wasn't home by 4:00am, so I started calling her, but her mobile was turned off. She got home around 5:00am and when I asked her where she had been for so long and why her mobile was turned off, instead of telling me the truth, she said that after the pool hall closed, they stayed outside talking and that she hadn't turned her mobile off, there was just no signal. Of course, I didn't believe her. We were both with the same service provider and I never had a problem with the signal in the pool hall.

The second time I caught her lying was when she was on holiday in Hungary with you kids, Krisztina and Attila, while I was working hard in Canada. I'm not sure if you remember, but because of my job I couldn't have holidays, especially not in the summer because that was the busiest time of the year, when I earned most of my money. But I sent you and your mother to Hungary for the whole summer, every summer.

Anyway, I think your mother thought that her relationship with this particular guy, who had worked for me before, was well established because a couple of weeks before the end of the summer, when I called her and you kids, she announced that she was leaving me. After more than eight years together and you two kids, she couldn't wait a few weeks to tell me this in person. I suddenly didn't know what to do, so I quickly bought a plane ticket to Hungary.

The flight was a week away, so in the meantime, I tried to reconcile with your mother by phone. I offered to leave you kids with your grandmother so your mother and I could go somewhere together. Of course, she didn't like the idea so she told me that her mother was very ill, so two of us going anywhere for a couple of days was out of the question. Curiously, the next time I called, she wasn't with you kids, she was spending a few days visiting a 'very good girlfriend' of hers, I think in Moson-magyaróvár. Of course, that wasn't true either, as she didn't know anyone in that city. Also, when I checked the phone bill I could see that she never made a single call to that city or any other. So, she wouldn't come anywhere with me for a few days, but for her 'very good girlfriend', whom she never called, she was able to leave her 'dying' mother for days. I knew she was going somewhere with some guy and just lying to me again. At that point I didn't know that it was the same guy. I, on the other hand, was glad to see that they were having fun at my expense. That guy was a dead beat. He worked here and there but he never really had any money, so I knew that I was funding their 'honeymoon'. It made me so happy, not.

After arriving in Hungary from Canada, I lingered for a few more days at your grandmother's place, Krisztina and Attila, where you kids and your mother were staying. Once again, I to tried to reconcile with your mother, but she was adamant and asked me to leave her alone and go to Szeged because she didn't want to spend her last days in Hungary with me.

So, that's what I did. I went to Szeged and stayed there

until it was time to fly back to Canada. More precisely, I went from Szeged to Kevermes, where my friend Laci (Anita's father) invited me to his silver wedding anniversary and there I met my real soul mate, Anita, but I will tell you kids about that in more detail later.

I bought a nice necklace in Szeged and when I went back to Canada, I think, Attila, it was you who remarked that the guy who worked for me had one just like it. I was very surprised that you knew this, because when we had last met this guy in Canada before he went to Hungary, he didn't have such a necklace then. He came back to Canada a week earlier than me, just like you kids and your mother, and when you, Attila, told me that we had the same necklace, we hadn't actually met the guy since our return from Hungary.

Then, Krisztina and Attila, I asked your mother if she was seeing this guy behind my back, but she lied again and said 'No'. She claimed that she had last seen him when we met him in Canada together before you kids went to Hungary with her and that since then she hadn't seen him. Of course, this wasn't true, because the next time I saw this guy, it turned out that he had also bought his necklace in Hungary and it was exactly like mine, which meant that your mother and you, Attila, must have met him when I wasn't around. At that time I wasn't sure if it was in Hungary too or just in Canada but I knew that your mother had been cheating on me with him. I was wrong. She had an ongoing affair with him which is kind of worse than just cheating and it was definitely worse than what I had done to her.

By the way, when I first met this guy in Canada, after we came back from Hungary, I became certain then that your mother was lying. It was at Frankie's place – he was a mutual friend. I was already with Anita and we were enjoying a peaceful drink with Frankie when someone rang the doorbell. Frankie went to see who it was and came back alone a few minutes later. When I asked 'Who was it?', he said 'It's the guy your ex had an affair with', but he said that he wasn't going to let him in, unless, I promised that I wouldn't hurt him.

I wasn't interested in your mother and her affairs at all by then, because I was in love with Anita, so I told Frankie he could let the guy in. Anyway, I wanted to talk to him to confirm my suspicions and find out the truth about what happened before your mother broke up with me. Unfortunately, kids, your mother was only able to lie to me so I was never able to find out the truth from her.

So, the guy came in and then he claimed that they were no longer together, but that their relationship had started in Canada and continued in Hungary. The pool hall, the 'very good girlfriend' in Hungary – that was him. He also told me that they met even after they came back from Hungary, while I was still there.

The next time I met your mother and confronted her with these facts, she still denied everything. I think she felt bad because I had only cheated on her once and had even admitted it, while she had an affair with this guy for months and lied continuously about it. Even though I caught her lying several times and her lover told me the whole story, she still carried on lying. So, I ask you kids, 'Who was more dishonest in our relationship?' Do I deserve to be banned from contacting you, Krisztina and Attila, while she enjoyed staying with you without any setbacks, despite her behaviour?

By the way, Krisztina and Attila, your mother recently approached Anita on Messenger and told her lies that even Anita knew were lies. She claimed that she never banned me from contacting you kids and that I was the one who didn't want to keep in touch with you. She told these lies to Anita, who has been with me since your mother kicked me out. Anita knows everything about how your mother behaved after our separation and how she ignored my phone calls, letters and emails. Anita knows exactly how much I cried and suffered because I couldn't keep in touch with you kids. Your mother even wrote to Anita to say how happy she would be if I were to contact you. I don't understand why your mother didn't contact me then, instead of Anita. Why didn't she write these things to me? Because again, she just wanted to fuck with me, just like before. How do I know that? Well, as soon as Anita asked for your phone number and told your mother that I would indeed like to contact you kids and how happy that would make me, your mother wrote straight back saying 'Krisztina has no phone and Attila lives with me.' At least half of this is lies again, for sure, because I can't believe you don't have a phone, Krisztina. If it's true, Attila, that you live with your mother and don't have a mobile phone either, then she could have given her own mobile number to Anita, so I could call you. After that, whatever Anita wrote to your mother, she didn't respond.

I will write about our relationship with your mother later. You can find out in more detail what your mother was like after our divorce and also why I was banned from contacting you and why she poisoned your minds against me. Kids, please believe that I desperately want to keep in touch with you. Look, I've even written a book now just to see if fate brings us together this way. Surely that counts for something!

I know kids that I didn't spend too much time with you, because that 10 and 7 years, compare to a lifetime I wanted to spend with you is almost nothing but whatever time I spent with you kids, was a gift. I always wish for more but I know that I should cherish what we had. I shouldn't be insatiable, right? As much as it broke my heart that I couldn't keep in touch with you, I never thought it might have been better if I didn't even get to know your mother and wouldn't have you because that way I have never met you kids. And I wouldn't give that up for the world. That little time we spent together was one of my best times in my life. No matter the length of the time we spent together, the only thing matter is the quality of that time.

I still live my life by this code that not the length of the life matters but the quality of it because this way if I die tomorrow I wouldn't have any regrets and I die happy.

CHAPTER TWENTY-THREE

I WANNA BE YOUR BOYFRIEND

At first I didn't take Anita seriously. The truth is, based on the picture that Anita's dad, Laci showed me, her sister was better looking, but Viki and Mimi, let me tell you how I met your mother.

After my future ex-wife kicked me out and I went to Hungary where I failed to reconcile with her, I complied with Anita's dad's invitation and went to his silver wedding. He had been married to Anita's mother, Veronka, for 25 years. The way I met Anita was like a fairy tale, at least I like to think so, but it's certainly miraculous. When Laci invited me, we were in Canada and I still believed that my relationship with my future ex-wife was going well. I know now that I was mistaken. How happy I thought I was. The first time Laci invited me to his silver wedding, I said no because I thought that everything was fine between me and my future ex-wife. I had no idea what a wonderful change this invitation would bring to my life. I don't believe in God, but I think there's something that controls our lives and directed mine to Anita.

Since my 'dear' future ex-wife didn't want to reconcile with me, it was time for Plan B: hook up with as many girls as possible, have lots of sex and don't get serious with anyone. This plan didn't work out very well for me because the first girl I met was Anita and luckily, I am still with her to this day. But enough talking: here are the details.

I was drinking like a fish with my friends in Szeged. I didn't plan to go to Laci's silver wedding in a small village called Kevermes, but because of booze and ecstasy, I changed my mind on a whim. It was morning and everyone was as drunk as the night before. Since I couldn't sleep because of the ecstasy I had taken, I decided to borrow a car from someone and go to Kevermes. I have to add that I didn't even know where Kevermes was and where I was going to get a car from.

I poked my drunken friends and my best friend Lacika said that maybe his brother Gabi could lend me one. Regardless of my condition, I went to Gabi's flat.

Lacika and his family may not remember me the way I remember them, but the whole family treated me as if I was one of them, as if I was a fourth brother. Lacika had two brothers. True, this was a long time ago before I escaped from the military and left Hungary, but regardless, I still have a huge fondness for the whole family. Lacika's mum 'cured' me countless times when I had a hangover and believe me, it was many times.

Anyway, Gabi lent me his car. So we can say that I kind of owe him because I probably wouldn't have met Anita without his generosity. The way I was looking that morning, he could easily have said 'I'm not lending my car to you because you're still drunk and your eyes look like you haven't slept for a week', but he said 'Yes'. It was a Kispolszki (126 Polski Fiat) but I got it. Everything was fine, I just didn't know where Kevermes was. First, I stopped at a petrol station to refuel and to buy a map, but then I couldn't restart the engine. To my shame, I had to ask the petrol station attendant for help. The guy just laughed at how clueless I was. He climbed into the car, reached down between the two front seats and pulled the 'starting lever'. After that, I was flying towards

Kevermes.

I knew there was a party in Kevermes, but I didn't know where. As I was/am a resourceful kind of guy, I immediately went to the local boozer to ask the locals. Luckily, the local postman drank at that boozer and he knew where the party was.

I turned up at the address and I didn't know anybody there apart from Anita's father, Laci, and our mutual friend, Feri. I first met Feri in Canada and through him I met Anita's father, Laci. A friend of mine came to me one day saying that her friend just moved to Toronto from Montreal and was looking for a job. I almost always needed extra help so I hired Feri and we became good friends. Floor fitting wasn't Feri's favoured choice of work, so he retrained as a flight attendant. Living in bilingual Montreal, he spoke fluent French as well as English. And then one day Feri came to me and asked if I would hire his family friend and that turned out to be Laci, Anita's father. I hired him too but floor fitting wasn't his best line of work either, because he was a painter and decorator. I had friends in that trade as well, so after a few phone calls I found Laci a job in his own trade. That's how I got closer and closer to Anita.

Anyway, let's get back to the party. To my great surprise, everyone was waiting for me. A few hours before I arrived, I hadn't even been sure I was coming but everyone had waited for me. I wondered how long they would have waited for me if I had decided to stay at home. However, as a punishment for being late, I had to drink a big glass of pálinka. Was that punishment? It remains the best one I have ever tasted in my life.

Everyone greeted me as if I had always been a family member. I had never before experienced this in my life. My future ex-wife's family hated me with a passion and I think their influence also contributed to my failed reconciliation with her. They hated me from the very beginning for no good reason. It could have been the way I looked. Who knows? On the other hand, everyone loved me in Kevermes. And that's when Anita and I got together. Our relationship began casually with lots of sex, but it developed into everlasting love.

Feri 'punishing' me with a big glass of 'pálinka'

I was just as honest in my relationships then as now, so I told Anita that I was a family man who had just got kicked out by his future ex-wife. I also told her that I still wanted to reconcile with her because we had children. However, I also told her that if that didn't work out, I would love to invite her to Canada. It was the best decision of my life. To this day, I remember when I first saw her at the airport in her brown jacket. Whenever I catch myself taking her for granted, I always think back to that moment.

There have been many girls in my life, but none are like Anita. I remember she was so shy in front of me at first, that she only got naked in the dark before having sex. But today, she is not ashamed to even fart in my presence. How far we have come! My dear Viki and Mimi, your mother was the sexiest chick I ever met. I will never forget the sight of her, after she finally overcame her shyness and stood a front of me in her little white thong and matching white bra in my room, where I grew up. After my future ex-wife kicked me out, I lost my mojo, but that sight immediately jump started my lust for life.

Anita (in her brown jacket), Krisztina, me & Attila taking the Toronto Maple Leafs on

Today, Kevermes is my favourite village, because it brought me together with Anita. After the silver wedding, we went to a night club in Gyula. Anita was completely attached to me. I understood, I was the best looking guy in the neighbourhood. I write this not only because it is about me, but because it was true. Anita was the same in a female version. I was even dancing with her, which I really don't like, just to be with her as much as possible. We kissed a lot and had a great time.

The last time I was in Gyula I didn't have such a good experience, because then we were beaten up. My brother had a girlfriend there and that's why we went there – my brother, Rubber and I. I don't remember exactly why we didn't meet my brother's girlfriend and how we ended up in a disco, but I do remember picking up a couple of girls. Of course, the local 'cool' guys didn't like it and when we escorted the girls home, they came after us, about six of them in one car. Rubber and I were knocked down relatively quickly and got kicked on the ground, but my brother was different. They had trouble with him because he wasn't afraid to use anything to win a fight. My brother had a knife that also had a reamer on it. My brother clenched his knife into his fist so that the reamer was sticking out between his fingers and he hit the jerks with it. By the end, four arseholes were attacking my brother, but they still couldn't beat him. My brother cut some of their faces, arms and legs open with the reamer. He just hit them wherever he could. They began to shout, 'Watch out he's going to kill us!', and my brother replied, 'Yes, I will kill you jerks!' Then the bastards shat their pants, jumped back into the car and drove away. Like I said, it wasn't as nice as with Anita, but it happened.

Anyway, let's get back to Anita and to our pleasant night. The evening is a bit of a blur in my memory, because I hadn't slept the night before and by the time we came out of the disco, I had been drinking and taking ecstasy for two days, but I remember spending that night in Gyula at the flat of one of Anita's relatives. I also remember that I tried to convince Anita to cuddle with me and continue the evening in one bed, but unfortunately, despite my best efforts, our first night together was spent in separate beds.

The next morning, we went back to Szeged. Anita's parents stayed in Kevermes, so their flat was empty and we had it to ourselves. We took advantage of that. We bought food, booze and continued where we had left off the night before. My hometown Szeged seems to be a luckier place than Gyula, because I managed to convince Anita there and sweeten her into my bed. Well, actually it was her parents' bed but it doesn't matter. Finally, after many years, I had normal, enjoyable sex in my life again. When my future ex-wife had sex with me every now and then, it wasn't normal sex either. I just called it a 'mercy fuck' because she just lay on her back and allowed me to climb on her. Many times, jerking off felt better.

So this, dear Viki and Mimi, is how I met your mother. I'll write more about our adventures together later. We've been together for over twenty years now and you two were only born six and eight years after we met and a lots of things happened to us before then.

CHAPTER TWENTY-FOUR

TODAY YOUR LOVE, TOMORROW THE WORLD

After I failed to reconcile with my future ex-wife, in the summer of 1999 I asked Anita to come to Canada. I paid for her open ticket and said if she didn't like it she could go back to Hungary any time. So she came to Canada in November 1999 and we celebrated 2000 together.

Me & Anita before we began our serious relationship (just boyfriend & girlfriend)

She was studying back in Hungary, so we had to keep flying back to Hungary for her exams. She also got work in Canada, cleaning houses. My work was flexible too, so splitting our time between Canada and Hungary wasn't a problem that first year. Then she received permission to defer her studies, we went back to Canada and spent a whole year there together. It was a very good time. She was young and it was her first extended time outside of the Eastern bloc.

Árpi & me at Niagara Falls when we didn't have to worry about my future ex-wife anymore

After my future ex-wife kicked me out and Anita arrived in Canada, we moved to Feri's house. He was renting a two- bedroom flat but was only using one of the bedrooms. He was barely there, because as a flight attendant he spent at least 4–5 days away from home at a time. It was the perfect place for us. Feri had no problem with you, Krisztina and Attila, being there. You kids spent lots of nights there, especially when your mother had a boyfriend. Beside you kids, even my friends could come and visit me there.

I didn't want to get married, because my first marriage had failed, so Anita and I we were just girlfriend and boyfriend. At that time I was using lots of drugs, especially ecstasy. We went to a party every weekend and sometimes even during the week.

There was a 'Hungarian Club' too, where Hungarian musicians made guest appearances from time to time. My future ex-wife was a part of the team which organised these events. One weekend, Erika Zoltán and her husband Robby D were the guests. I went to the concert with Anita and other friends, regardless that I didn't know them. I met your mother there, and we spoke about you, Krisztina and Attila, and agreed that I would pick you kids up the next morning.

The next morning I knocked on the door but there was no answer. I could hear some movement from inside so I yelled 'Open the door. It's me. I'm here to pick up the kids'.

Then someone yelled back: 'There are no kids here'.

What? So I asked nicely: 'Who the fuck are you? What the hell are you doing in my flat? Where are my kids?'

The voice told me to 'Go away!'

I told the voice 'I'm calling the cops because you are in my flat, trespassing and don't want to open the door'. I called the cops. They asked me to give the trespasser one more chance to explain herself and what she was doing in my flat without my kids. They got scared from the cops and someone opened the door.

'Who are you?' I asked.

'I'm Erika Zoltán,' she said. I had seen her concert the night before but I didn't recognise her. Like I said kids, I didn't know her and the night before I was so wasted I wouldn't have recognised my own mother. So we started talking and they told me that your mother had given them the flat until their return to Hungary and she and you, Krisztina and Attila, were sleeping at her boyfriend's house.

'Jesus,' I said. She could have mentioned this when we met the night before.

There were about 5–6 people sleeping in my flat – Erika Zoltán, her husband Robby D and some backup dancers. After the bad start, things improved. They apologised for not opening the door but your mother had told them not to open the door to anyone. They poured me a glass of whisky and we talked for about half an hour. They were nice people but got scared, just like me, when we didn't know what was happening.

Krisztina and Attila, when your mother got a boyfriend, it was our best times together, because then sometimes I could have you kids even for a whole week. She seemed to have a different boyfriend every other week when I went to pick you up. I don't know how you kids could learn their names, they rotated so quickly. But when she didn't have a boyfriend, if I was five minutes late bringing you kids home, she screamed my head off.

When she kicked me out, we agreed that we would not force you kids to come with me on the weekends. If you wanted to come you could come, if you didn't, you wouldn't have to.

Attila, you came with me the first time but Krisztina, you didn't. I know your mother told you to 'Stay home with me otherwise I'll be so lonely' because you told me that later. She was doing the same thing as her mother did to her brother. Of course, your grandmother was lonely. No man could live with her 'attitude'. She chewed up two men in her life and then started a campaign of 'emotional terror' on her own son so he would stay with her. She wasn't lonely any more but poor son, he didn't even have a girlfriend when I knew him and he was more than 20 years old. Krisztina and Attila, I'm sorry to say it, but your mother is just the same.

Hungarians have a saying: 'Look at the mother, marry her daughter'. Now I know how true this is. Just like your grandmother, kids, as your mother told Anita just recently, your mother is lonely and I believe if you, Attila, still live with her then she is doing the same thing as her mother did to her brother. On the other hand, look at Anita's parents. They were together as they promised: 'until death do us part.' My parents were the same. They were together until my mother died. And look at Anita and I, over twenty years now and still counting.

Anyway, let's get back to the first day when you, Krisztina, wanted to come with us to see a movie. You were afraid to tell your mother but when Anita and I arrived to pick up Attila, you told me that you wanted to come with us. Even then, after we had agreed with your mother if you kids want to come she has to let you come, even then, she said 'Krisztina you can't go'.

I replied 'What? That wasn't our agreement. Of course she can come'.

Your mother, Krisztina, was looking at you as if she was going to die if you came with us and asked you 'You really want to go?' hoping that after this pressure you would say 'no' but luckily, you said 'Yes, I really want to go with Dad'. After that weekend you came with us every time. We had so much fun. We always went somewhere interesting, either just for a day trip or camping for a week. We spent a lot of time together in Hungary as well in the summer of 2001 and 2002.

I don't understand, kids, how come you don't remember those days. How can you think I'm a bad guy or father? I'm the same as I was then. Only your mother says bad things about me because her life didn't turn out the way she planned and now she is probably jealous because my life turned out great with Anita, Viki and Mimi.

Anyway, dear Krisztina and Attila, in January 2000 I finally got divorced from your mother – aka my future ex-wife – so from now on I proudly can call her my ex-wife.

Besides going on trips with you kids, I went with friends as well. Once Miki, Frankie and I rented a cabin by a lake which was so far up North that there was no road to it. We drove to the farthest lake where the road ended and from there we flew north in a seaplane to the remote lake where we had rented a cabin. I even flew the plane for about 10–15 minutes. I sat beside the pilot when we were boarding the plane so when we were in the air and there was nothing around us, the pilot let me control the plane. The plane had dual controls so I was able to fly it in complete safety.

First, the pilot gave me some instructions and a few minutes later I was flying the plane. Don't get me wrong, it's not a big deal. Anybody can do it but not everybody has a chance to do it. So we landed on our own lake (there was only our cabin by that lake) on a Saturday afternoon and the pilot left us and told us that he would be back on Wednesday to see if we needed anything. Until then, we were on our own – there would be no communication with the outside word.

After the pilot left, we started drinking right away and we were joking about what would happen if one of us got seriously injured. By Wednesday we could be dead. At the cabin everything worked on gas as there was no electricity. By 'everything', I mean the gas cooker and the fridge. We had a kayak and a motor boat by the lake and lots of fuel. There were some rules posted on the wall of the cabin, the most important of which was that we shouldn't leave any food out and if we caught a fish we had to take the fish guts to the other side of the lake otherwise bears could attack us.

It was a fishing trip but Miki and Frankie brought some guns too. I told them that if there was an accident I didn't think I could help because I usually faint when I see blood, especially if it's mine. They were laughing at me and reassured me that there would be no accident. But, of course, they were wrong.

I think it was on the very first day that we started to play with an axe that Miki had brought. We tried to throw the axe into the tree's trunk from about ten metres away. Frankie and I did it a few times but Miki just couldn't. I forgot to mention that we were drunk as hell of course. For us it was normal to play a mortally dangerous game totally pissed at the end of the world, where there was no medical help. Anyway, it was Miki's turn and he missed the tree again. He got so upset that he grabbed the axe, went to the tree and without letting the axe go he tried to stick it into the trunk. He was so pissed that he couldn't hit the tree properly with the axe, not even so close, so the axe glanced off the trunk into his fucking leg. Right into his fucking shinbone. Frankie was so brave, he ran into the woods right away and he didn't come out for about an hour.

Miki begged me to 'Do something!' so I stared at him nervously but the axe was still in his leg. Fuuuuuck! I felt very weak but because Frankie had run away and there was no one else, I had to help him. I got the first aid kit from the cabin and removed the axe from his leg. I can't remember whether we had some kind of disinfectant fluid or if I used vodka, but I poured something on the wound and put a bandage on it. Luckily, before we left I had visited my GP and had told him where we were going and he had given me some strong painkillers and some pills for infection. Miki took the medications and drank heavily until Wednesday when the plane arrived and he was taken to the nearest hospital. He returned the next day. Fortunately, because of the medications and the frequent changes of bandages, he hadn't suffered any serious or permanent damage.

We also went bear hunting but the bears were much smarter than us so we didn't see any. We saw their footprints on the other side of the lake where we left the fish guts so we knew that they were around but they hid from us very well.

We didn't have a proper toilet just an outhouse. We had a rifle and a pistol too, so when we went to the outhouse we always took the pistol just in case a bear should turn up. I don't think that pistol would been any match for a bear but we liked to think so. One time, I was in the outhouse doing number two, when I heard noises coming from outside. It sounded like someone or something was coming through the woods towards the outhouse. It was lucky I was on the toilet, because otherwise I would have shat my pants. I was afraid to go out so I waited and waited but whatever that thing was, it was still making noise. Fearing for my life, I slowly opened the door. I peeked out and I saw a huge family of squirrels frolicking around.

The rest of our trip was peaceful. We did target practice, fished, kayaked and raced around in the motor boat. At night we built a camp fire and cooked some food on it. It was so dark at night that if we went about ten metres from the fire we couldn't see it but then millions of stars revealed themselves in the night sky. It was so quiet. There was no other noise except the forest or the lake and the animals who lived there. It was breathtaking.

At the start of the summer of 2000 in June after Anita had finished her last exam, we were ready to go back to Canada. We bought the tickets to arrive on my birthday on the 14th. My brother picked us up from the airport and took us home. We dropped our bags, took a quick shower, put on some clean clothes and we were ready to party. Actually, there was a party in Oakville at a friend's place but before we went there we stopped at a bar to get something to eat. We ordered a pitcher of beer because twenty chicken wings came free with it. After finishing the first one we ordered another because we were still 'hungry'. In the mean time, we had a few shots too. We were celebrating my 33rd birthday and our arrival in Canada. Anita wasn't drinking, so my brother and I could have as many drinks as we wanted but because we were still heading to a party later, we stopped after the second pitcher. Then Anita started whining that she didn't want to go to the party and she wasn't willing to drive us there.

'Come on, don't be a twat', I said, 'It's my birthday!'

My polite approach didn't change her mind so I got behind the wheel and we took off to Oakville. I had no problem driving, I wasn't that drunk. I'd had a good time with my brother, whom I hadn't see for weeks and it was my birthday, so I figured if we went to the party, maybe by the end of it Anita would have changed her mind and drive us home. As usual, I figured wrong because on the way to the party the cops stopped me and charged me for DUI. I'm still not sure why they pulled us over because I didn't do anything wrong. My best guess would be that we were young, I was driving a big Cadillac DeVille with three of us sitting in the front. We were also singing along to very loud music, so the cops thought we were up to no good. Still, they didn't have the right to pull us over unless we had broken the law. They were in an unmarked car, so we didn't spot them but it shouldn't have mattered because we hadn't done anything wrong. After my breathalyser registered me over the limit, they lied so they could charge me. Motherfuckers. They claimed that they had been following us for about 10 minutes and that on one occasion I had changed lane very quickly.

On the report I received, they said that I had changed lane right behind them at an unsafe distance. Both claims were bullshit. A lawyer told me later that if it had happened in Toronto, the judge would have thrown my case out. But because of my 'good luck', I stood trial in the small town of Burlington.

As if my luck wasn't bad enough, at that time Canada had let a lots of Hungarian gypsies into the country as ethnic refugees and of course, they were only criminals and committed so much crime that they were in the news every day. As soon as the judge realised I was Hungarian, he just fucked me. He suspended my driving licence for a year. And if you kids think that was all, you are mistaken. When I got to the court house with Anita, two cops came up to me and they said 'We want to talk to you'. Believe me, kids, when the police came up to me to talk it was never good. We went into a small room – like an interrogation room – a female cop sat across the table and the male, who was as big as a mountain, stood blocking the door.

'Holy shit', I thought, I'm in big trouble.

'Have you used any other name in Canada?' asked the female cop, as she dropped three folders in front of me with three different names on them: B. Volker, Lacika and mine. Technology had finally caught up with me. The cops had taken my fingerprints when they caught me for DUI and by then all fingerprints were digitised and in the system.

For some reason, the system couldn't match old fingerprints but as soon as they put my fingerprints in the system, two other names came out. The cops didn't know which one was my real name and who I was and that's why they questioned me before my trial. I realised that lying would be foolish so I told her that I had used B. Volker's name and passport to get to Canada because I couldn't get a passport on my own name because I had escaped from the Hungarian military. I used Lacika's name after that because until Hungary gave me an amnesty, I could still be sent to jail for a long time if Canada should extradite me. I used my own name after I got amnesty, which was the plan from the beginning. I told her that I had already applied for permanent residency and that I had mentioned all of this on my application because I wanted to clear my name. I told her that I was using Lacika's name and driving licence because I hadn't cleared my name yet and I didn't have any documents in my own name. Of course, this wasn't true but they couldn't prove otherwise, so they had to let me go.

That wasn't the end of it, because they sat in the court room when my trial was on and the female cop wouldn't stop yelling to the judge that I had used different names and that the name I was using even then was not my real name. Luckily, the judge got tired of her and told her 'Sit down and be quiet. If what you're saying is true, then make a case of it and bring him back to trial. Right now we are here for his DUI and for nothing else.' She shut up after that and both of them left the court room before the end of my trial. I was afraid that they were waiting outside to re-arrest me, so I sent Anita out first to see where they were but they had left, so we got home safely.

CHAPTER TWENTY-FIVE

WE'RE A HAPPY FAMILY

After that year in Canada, we went back to Hungary with Anita so that she could resume her studies. During that whole time while I was in Canada with her, I could still see you kids, even though your mother had custody. I gave her the condo and everything in it. I took my car, she took hers and I took my working van, which I later sold for the amount I owed to the bank. But she had everything else.

Attila, me & Krisztina the last time when we were together & happy together, 'imádlak'

During Spring Break 2003, I went to visit you, Krisztina and Attila, in Canada. I had no idea that this would be the last time I would see you.

Before that Spring Break I had no problem talking to you kids. Your mother always answered my calls and gave the phone to you so we could catch up with what had happened to each of us. That Spring Break was fun. I again took you to many places and we slept at Feri's again. I even took you to the Hungarian School on a Saturday. I was surprised that your mother let me do that, but I soon realised why.

When I was dropping you kids off, a young Hungarian couple approached me. I didn't know them but they knew you kids and they knew your mother too, of course. They asked me where your mother was. I told them that she was probably at home. They asked if I could talk to her because she wasn't answering their calls. They wanted her to call them because she had borrowed $1,500 from them that she was supposed to have paid back weeks earlier. The young couple were moving back to Hungary in the next few days and they really needed that money. I told them 'I can try but she is really just my kids' mother and no one to me'.

After them, another guy came to talk to me. I knew him from before; he was a nice guy and your mother's boyfriend. You kids even lived together in his house with his two sons while your mother rented out the condo. Even Anita and I were invited once for one of your birthday parties. You looked happy. This guy had a booming painting and decorating business and he was making very good money. His wife had left him so he was also happy to have found a new partner in your mother.

Anyway, he told me that he also wanted to talk to your mother because he couldn't reach her either. He told me that they were now separated but while they were together he had leased a car for your mother and made the payments himself. When they separated, they agreed that your mother could keep the car but that she had to take over the payments.

I think you kids can guess what happened. Your mother didn't make the payments. So this poor guy was receiving phone calls and letters from the bank threatening to repossess the car if he didn't pay. That was why he wanted to talk to your mother but of course, your mother knew that so she just ignored him. I told the poor guy the same thing I told the young couple. I know from you, Krisztina, that the car was repossessed some time later because you wrote me an email after the bank took the car back. You wrote 'Someone took our car and they still want us to pay'. You didn't know, but it wasn't your mother who had to pay but that poor guy who helped your mother out and signed the lease. Anyway, when I saw your mother the next time I confronted her with this problem but like any other time, she denied the whole thing and just lied. I even told her that if she had money problems and couldn't keep up with the mortgage payments and condo fees, then we should sell the condo.

I spoke to the agent who sold the condo to us and he told me that the condo was worth $180,000 even in the worst condition. But the condo was in good condition so we probably could have got more than that. By then the outstanding mortgage on the condo was around $80,000–85,000 so even with the selling costs we would have been left with about $90,000. I told your mother that she could keep all the money if you guys would move back to Hungary. I didn't even care which city – just so long as it was Hungary.

With that sum of money at that time, your mother could easily have bought a house. It was a good plan. I was in Hungary, so we could have seen each other more often and I could have helped you better. Your mother obviously wasn't doing very well in Canada, so she had no reason to stay and nothing to lose. Of course, your mother didn't like my plan. She told me that her money problems were temporary and that she would solve them shortly. She said that she didn't want to sell the condo because that was your inheritance.

I knew that her money problems were not temporary but I couldn't sell the condo by myself. I also knew that your mother just didn't want to sell the condo because that would have meant that I was right when she kicked me out, and I told her that she would not to be able to keep up with all the payments and provide you kids with the same lifestyle as I did. This decision of hers and what followed is the reason why your mother didn't let us keep in touch. Her selfishness ruined all three of us. Anyway, the Spring Break was over and my time was up, so I went back to Hungary.

When I arrived safely in Hungary, I tried to call you kids but there was no answer, so I left a message. Your mother didn't call me back, so I called again a few days later. No answer again, so I left a message but your mother didn't call me back. This went on for a few weeks until I received a phone call from – my supposed friend – Miki. You kids remember him, right? I had many adventures with him. My pills and my care 'at the end of the world' probably saved his life when he had the accident with the axe. He told me that your mother didn't want to move to Hungary but she did want to sell the condo, so I should sign everything over to her so she could do that. He also said 'And as soon as 'we' sell the condo 'we'll' give you $10,000'.

'What the fuck are you talking about, Miki?' I said. 'You are one of my best friends. You have nothing to do with the condo so don't fucking say 'we' and act like you do. She turned down my offer just a few weeks ago when I was in Canada and since I came back to Hungary she hasn't answered my phone calls, so I can't talk to my kids. Even now, she doesn't have the guts to call me. I'm not going to sign anything'.

Miki told me that your mother was stressed out and

depressed and she couldn't deal with this either. But, kids, knowing how your mother turned out, all the rip offs, all the lies I knew this was a scam. I knew that Miki had just sold his house because of his divorce so he had money. I told him that I would sign all the paperwork I had to so your mother could sell the condo, but that I wanted the money upfront. I told him that I would send the papers to Feri and he could pick them up as soon as he had brought the $10,000.

So I sent the papers to Feri, but instead of bringing the money, Miki brought the cops. He told them that Feri had important documents that didn't belong to him. When the cops knocked on Feri's door and told him why they were there, Feri called me right away for instructions. I told him not to open the door no matter what they said unless they had a search warrant. But I knew that they didn't have that.

I told Feri to explain the situation to the cops through the door. He did that and the cops left right away. Fucking Miki betrayed me for my ex. Fucking traitor. But I think he got what he deserved because I figured your mother borrowed money from him to pay the missed mortgage payments and condo fees and promised him that as soon as I signed the papers and they had sold the condo, she would give him the money back.

They might even had an affair and wanted to live together in the condo and they wanted me out of the way. I don't know. The only thing I know for sure that I would never seen a penny from the condo if I sign the papers.

After the cops left, Miki stayed there and kicked Feri's door for a while, screaming and yelling for the papers, so I told Feri 'Burn the papers and tell Miki to fuck off otherwise you will call the cops'. If Miki hadn't had his money invested in the condo he wouldn't have been so angry; he would have had nothing to lose and that's how I know that your mother ripped him off too.

Anyway, as soon as he knew that Feri had burned the papers and was willing to call the cops, Miki left. And that, kids, is the reason why your mother didn't let us talk or write to each other. She couldn't scam me so we all had to suffer. You kids had to grow up thinking that your father didn't want anything to do with you because of this.

Shame on your mother. She knew how much I loved you and knew how much I'd suffer and she also knew how much you kids would suffer, but she didn't care as long as she had the satisfaction of making my life miserable. She also figured that as long as she continued to lie to you kids, telling you that every financial and emotional problem you had in your life was because of me, she would be OK. So she blamed everything on me.

While you kids were young and all the commun-ications had to go through your mother, then it was easy for her to ignore my phone calls, not to tell you kids about my emails and throw out my letters. In the mean time, she poisoned your minds against me so when you got old enough to contact me, you just didn't want to.

Who can blame you? I'm sure I don't. It was inevitable that you should think: 'Why should we try to find our 'old man' when he ignored us and wanted nothing to do with us when we were growing up? Fuck him'. Anyway, I can't say this enough: I'm writing this book to let you kids – all four of you – know that I'm here for you, so please don't be a stranger.

This next story happened when we didn't have you Viki and Mimi yet and we were living temporarily with Anita's parents because we were looking for a flat. I was going 'home' from a company party and on the way I went into a boozer near where Anita's parents lived. I was newly returned to Hungary, so I didn't know which boozers to avoid. Unfortunately, as you kids guessed, this boozer was one of them.

Me & Lacika reuniting in Szeged after many many years

I ordered one drink and I woke up the next morning, outside on a bench with my ear bleeding and my watch and necklace missing.

I didn't know and I still don't know what exactly happened but I'll give you my best guess. The bartender put something in my drink and I passed out. After that, I think he called his friends to came and take me out of the boozer acting like they were my friends and just wanted to take me home. They took me outside, set me on the bench and robbed me. I think that I probably looked like I was going to wake up so they hit my head on the bench and that was why my ear was bleeding. And it wasn't just bleeding, the cartilage was broken, so now I have cauliflower ear just like wrestlers have.

Now every time I meet someone new and they see my ear they always ask 'Did you used to be a wrestler?' 'Yes' I say all the time because it's true. I wrestled for about 2–3 months when I was young but it was not the cause of my cauliflower ear.

So my new life in Hungary began with Anita, with no children. We rented a small place and we got a job that paid the bills. We had fun. I had no responsibilities again, so it was superficially good, even though I was desperate to see you, Krisztina and Attila.

Rubber, Imi & me before my cauliflower ear happened

And on the 10th June 2005 you were born Viki on the third best day of my life.

Viki, 'imádlak'

We got married a few weeks later on 2nd July, which was also my mother's birthday but this was just a coincidence. It also coincided with a government initiative: anyone having two kids in five years received 2.5 million forints (about £8,000) towards a newly built flat or house. At that time you could buy a flat in Hungary for 12–15 million forints, so that was good money. But you had to be married to benefit from this government scheme, so that's why we got married. We bought a small flat in Szeged.

About a year after we moved in, the fourth best day of my life arrived on 5th May 2007, when you, Mimi, were born.

Mimi 'imádlak'

I love you kids and that's why I don't understand my father. While I was in Hungary, I visited him, first with Anita and then after you kids were born, with you, Viki and Mimi too, but he never came to visit us. I don't think he ever saw the flat we bought in Szeged but even if he did visit, it was maybe once.

He lived with his evil partner Marika in the same flat my brother and I grew up in. She always acted nice but she was a bad actor so we could see that she was just taking advantage of my alcoholic father. She was renting a small flat when she met my father but after a short while she moved in with him. She received a small pension but it was about a fifth of what my father received and she knew that my father's flat was mortgage free.

Every time we visited my father he complained about losing money, either in the pub or on the way home and that never used to happen to him before. He wasn't losing money; evil Marika stole it from him whenever he passed out at home.

We had a garage and a small hobby garden not far from our home. When we were young, my father used to repair cars in that garage and he rented it out when we got older. The small hobby garden was about a 10–15 minute ride away by bicycle and it had a small shed with electricity and a drilled well. We grew vegetables and fruits there and we used to cook food on the fire we made. In the shed there was a bed we could sleep on if we got tired after lunch. After we grew up, we used to go there with friends and cook food and drink a lot. I loved that little garden.

When we were kids, our father told us that one of us would inherit the garage and the other the garden. It was a good plan, so my brother chose the garden and I chose the garage. No argument there. Unfortunately, unlike the flat, the garden and the garage was in my father's name only, so after my mother died, my brother and I only inherited my mother's half of the flat.

When I bought our flat in Szeged, I needed some money for the deposit so I asked my father to sell the garage (my inheritance). I was waiting for some money from Canada but I wasn't sure if it was going to get to me in time. My father refused to sell it because he said 'Your ex-wife took your condo from you and I don't want the same thing to happen again with Anita'. You see, kids, there is a big differences between alcoholics. My father was a bad one. He didn't understand that I didn't leave the condo in Canada to my ex-wife, I left it to you, Krisztina and Attila, so you kids would have a decent place to live. How could he understand? To understand this, he would have had to love my brother and me. But he was always about the money. We had very different views of the world. I was and I still am about family rather than money.

Anyway, evil Marika stole so much money from my father that he had to sell the garage to keep up with the payments.

Once my father refused to give money to evil Marika's son to come to England to work. My father thought he wouldn't find work, just spend his money and return home after it was all gone. So evil Marika stole the money from my father and give it to her son. As my father had predicted, he returned to Hungary within a month. Then my father got angry and asked me to make him a will in which he left everything to my brother and me. So I did what he asked, but when it came to signing it, he refused and accused me of being selfish for cutting evil Marika off. I told him that I did this only because he asked me. He called me a liar even after Anita confirmed that she was there when he asked me. He later sold the hobby garden as well but neither my brother nor I got any money from it.

Nevertheless, I continued to involve him in our lives. I didn't break off our relationship but every time I tried to include him he always made excuses. When we had your christening, Mimi, we called my father and invited him. He refused, saying that he was very sick. I told him that he should be there because he is my father and your grandfather. I even offered to pick him up, take him to the restaurant for the celebration only and not to the church, which is boring and then to drive him back home because he complained about his legs, but he even refused to do that. Despite that, a few weeks later he travelled to another city to attend a graduation ceremony for evil Marika's grandson. He wasn't even related to him, but he took a bus to another city to attend that graduation.

The one thing I never managed to do while I was in Hungary was to mend my relationship with my father. When I lived in Canada, I had a lot more than him and he still acted like he was a better person. He never once told me that he was proud of me, even when I was leading a comfortable life. He always acted as though he hated me all the time.

Even though, I went back to school too. Education was the only thing where my father was ahead of me because he graduated from his vocational high school. You remember, kids, I left Vedres István Vocational High School of Building and Construction in its third year. But at the age of 33 I chose a different school which gave me higher education but no profession. Instead of a vocational high school I went to a grammar school. Luckily, I only had to finish the last two years because they accepted my two completed years at Vedres István Vocational High School.

This time, I was determined that nothing was going to stop me from graduating, albeit twenty years later than it should have been. I was one of the best in my class with only a few 4s and lots of 5s. And I even went further. I went to higher education to be a teacher but it cost a lots of money so I only completed the first term. Of course, my father wasn't impressed.

Anyway, I continued to wait for the money from the sale of the condo. As I predicted, Krisztina and Attila, your mother couldn't keep up with the payments, so the bank put the condo up for auction. Temporary money problem my arse! Of course, after the auction, we were only left with about $20,000 instead of the $90,000. Your mother preferred to deal with Miki rather than me even though that cost us about $70,000. Again, her hatred towards me cost you kids your decent lifestyle. She didn't care about hurting you, as long as she hurt me. Very sad. We could only get the money if both of us signed some documents and your mother didn't sign it for months just to screw me.

Money was tight, but we got by, it was just about enough to support the four of us. Then things went bad again. My wife, Anita, has a sister, who was married to Tamás Straubi and they had a son together. They were good friends of ours or so I thought. They tried to buy a car but were refused, so they asked me to buy the car and they agreed to pay for it. That's when the trouble started! We had very low interest on the loan (it was in Swiss franc), but it was tied into the Swiss franc exchange rate; if it went up, we would be in big trouble. It was risky, but they assured us that if anything went wrong they would sell their flat rather than leave us in shit because of them. So in November 2007 I bought them the car.

Sadly, their gamble didn't pay off. The Swiss franc exchange rate rocketed and the monthly payment for the car almost doubled within six months. The total cost of the car per month rose from 35,000 Hungarian forints (about £110) to 65,000 Hungarian forints (about £210), which was the same amount we were paying for our mortgage. It was a shitty car as well, nothing fancy – an Opel Astra (Vauxhall Astra in the UK). They couldn't afford to pay us the money, so I told them to sell their flat and pay off the loan completely, as they had originally promised but they refused. Fucking arseholes.

I hope, kids, you learn enough from me and at least you won't rip off your own family. This wanker, Tamás Staubi, always bad-mouthed my brother because he is an alcoholic. This piece of shit thought he was better than my brother because he almost never drank. But when my brother and I inherited 4 million Hungarian forints (about

£12,000) my brother refused to take his half because he said 'I'm an alcoholic and I'm making enough money to buy booze, I don't need more. You, brother, have family again and need the money more than I do, so keep it and spend it on your family'. Goodness and kindness has never been measured by the amount of alcohol people consume but by the way they act and behave towards others. So this ignorant bastard, Tamás Straubi, who thinks so much of himself is a no one in my eyes compared to my brother and to any of my alcoholic friends.

Anyway, I had to continue making the payments every month if I wanted to protect my good credit score and keep the car. After they missed a monthly payment, I called them up and told them that I couldn't afford to pay for their car because we were hardly getting by every month. I asked them to give the car back to me if they weren't going to sell their flat and buy it.

This fucking prick, Tamás Straubi, told me: 'Don't worry, we will pay you as soon as we can'. I replied, 'If my car is not here tomorrow I'll call the police and reported it stolen so don't fuck with me you fucking twat'. This fucking pussy, this spineless coward brought my car back the next day but he was so afraid of me that he parked it in front of Anita's father's garage and went home to Szigetszentmiklós just South of Budapest, without seeing me. After all this, they tried to convince the whole family that we were the bad relatives because this stupid idiot Tamás Straubi almost lost his job because he didn't have a car. What the fuck was this moron thinking? That I would pay for the car so he could go to work and not pay me back? Motherfucker! Of course, they didn't succeed, because everyone knew that we were right and the rest of the family loved me more than this stuck-up fuck.

Since then we don't keep in touch with them. They

never said sorry and never tried to make our relationship better even when they had the chance. Anita and her sister inherited 10 million Hungarian forints (about £28,000) after her parents died. Anita's sister could have offered some money from her 5 million Hungarian forints to try to make peace with us but she is just the same as her husband. In Hungary we have a saying: 'Every sack find its patch' and the way I see these two, it's true. They chose money rather than family.

So we had less and less money and we got into lots of debt. Every month, because of the car, we made less money than what we had to pay out. We ended up owing more than the equivalent of £5,000, which was a lots of money in Hungary.

CHAPTER TWENTY-SEX

I DON'T WANNA GO DOWN TO THE BASEMENT

So in September 2008, I came to the UK, with £350, the only money I could borrow at the age of 41, to start my life all over again. Anita and you kids, Viki and Mimi, you stayed in Hungary. I couldn't find a good job in Hungary, even though I could speak English. My old friend Árpi lived in Windermere, Cumbria as a live-in chef in a hotel restaurant, so he arranged for me to stay in the hotel at a discounted rate while I looked for work.

I traveled all over the Lake District with my CV looking for work. The pressure was really on me because my money was fast running out. Luckily, I found a job quickly. It was a live-in position as a kitchen porter in The Glen Rothay Hotel and Badger Bar in Rydal. I was peeling potatoes and carrots and washing the dishes – all the fun stuff. It was just a small hotel by the road in the middle of nowhere. The owner wasn't very nice so I found another job as a kitchen porter in The Priest Hole Restaurant in Ambleside. A few weeks after I started there, I became a waiter, which was a lot better and an easier job.

I popped back to Hungary to visit Anita and you girls as many time as I could and to see what was happening there but nothing had changed – I still couldn't afford to stay there. I even brought Anita with me once for a week to see the Lake District. Even as a kitchen porter I was earning enough money to send some back home. We started paying back our debts and then a Hungarian work colleague called Ernő lent me £4,000 to clear all of our debts in Hungary. I had worked with him from the start and we had become friends, but he wasn't rich. He was a chef, making better money than me, but he didn't really have the money to lend to me. In fact, he had applied for a loan for £2,000 and the bank had offered him £20,000 so he said thank you very much, took out the bigger loan and lent some of it to me.

I couldn't find a better job in the Lake District than restaurant or reception work, and I always had to work antisocial hours, evenings, early mornings, weekends. So I visited a friend who'd had enough of the USA and was working in London as a painter. I found a place to stay in London but it was a terrible area, so I visited Brighton instead. It was 2009 in the summer so it was very nice. I knew immediately that this was where I wanted to bring Anita and you girls. Many Hungarians were working there as street cleaners because they didn't speak English but it was a start for them. So I applied for the job and got it. I started work as a street cleaner in July and then at the end of the month I went back to Hungary to see Anita and you girls.

I actually flew to Budapest where I met Anita and you girls so you could come to England with me. From there we drove back to Brighton. We had no references, so we couldn't rent anywhere so were able to apply to the council. We we were given a council house rent-free on condition that we had to find alternative accommodation within six months. So that was a big help because we were able to put more money aside while not paying any rent. We saved up enough money for a six-month deposit and had a reference by then, too.

We signed a contract on a rented property and were able to give the landlord six months' rent upfront. He was very happy with us. After our six months was up, we signed a contract for another year, but he allowed us to pay monthly this time.

We were living in that flat when I bought an electronic drum kit for you girls because I always wanted to become a drummer, but it didn't work out so I thought that maybe my dream could come true through you. I was wrong. You girls hardly played on it. I tried to learn how to play the drums but it was too hard and I was lazy. Then my old friend Imi's son, our godson, Kristóf, started to play on it. Every time he visited us, he played it. In fact, he liked it so much that he started to take lessons.

When we moved across the street from them, he was there even more often, so I gave him the drum kit so he could practice any time he wanted. Since then he became so good that he had to sell my drum kit and buy a better one so he could improve further. Now he's playing in a group. My dream didn't come through you girls, but at least it came through Kristóf. He is family too, and I'm very proud of him.

Kristóf before

239

Kristóf now

Me, Imi, Kristóf, Anita, Mimi & Viki before the Brighton Eye was
taken down

In 2010 I started a plumbing course in City College
Brighton and Hove. I finished it in 2012, but after that it

took me another year to get the NVQ. While I was doing the course, I started working with a female plumber called Ruthie and became self-employed. Since then, I've been a plumber working for myself.

When the owner sold the flat, we moved to another one in the same building. It was around that time that you, Viki, started asking us for a dachshund. We told you that we couldn't buy a dog while we were living in a flat, so we bought you a black and tan soft toy dachshund and you named him Charlie.

Anita found a bungalow in the area, so we gave up the flat and moved there, and then you, dear Viki, didn't stop asking for a dog. So I gave in and looked around for a dachshund. They were very expensive in England, so I asked the parents of our other godson, Zétény, to look for two dachshund puppies in Hungary, a boy of course, and a girl. I thought maybe if she had puppies, we could sell them. The boy would have to have been black and tan to match your soft toy dachshund, Viki, but the girl could have been any colour.

When Zétény's parents found the puppies, I went back to Hungary to pick them up. I was there for a month to take care of all the necessary paperwork and even Anita and you girls came for a week in your half term. Actually, we picked up Charlie together. You girls named the girl puppy Caramella, because of her colour. Since then we got another girl, Coco, and we kept one of her daughters too, Delilah. Our family just got bigger and bigger in England.

Unfortunately, back in Hungary, it was the opposite. First Anita's mother and then my father died. I used to call my father many times from England, and we visited him every time we went to Hungary. Unfortunately, while I was in England, he died alone, without family, with only evil Marika at his side. She inherited everything, which I suspect was why she was there at all.

Charlie, Dee Dee (Delilah), Coco & Caramella waiting to bite me in the ass

After my mother died, my brother and I owned half the flat that my father lived in and he owned the other half. I didn't find out about his death for several months, because every time I phoned, evil Marika answered and pretended he was still alive and always told me he was out walking the dog.

After about three months and several phone calls, my father was still walking the dog. Then Anita's father died, so she went back to Hungary and I asked her to check on my father. When Anita went to see my father, evil Marika told her that my father was walking the dog. Anita didn't believe her so she told evil Marika that she would wait for my father. Then, and only then, did evil Marika admit that my father had died three months earlier and that he had been in hospital for several weeks before that.

Evil Marika had kept up her pretence because she thought we'd sell the flat to someone else to get the money for our half and then she would have had nowhere to go because she didn't have the money to buy us out. That is why I call her evil Marika. I wouldn't have kicked her out, but because of what she did, I told her that we would sell the flat and she could either buy us out or she'd have to move. I don't understand why she did it because there was no hatred between us and we seemed to get on fine.

Neither I nor my brother wanted to go back there to live in that flat. Because of her stupidity and greediness or whatever we can call her behaviour, I was unable to say goodbye to my father. Poor bastard. At the end, evil Marika's son – who ran an electrical shop – bought us out. So there was no reason for her to have acted the way she did.

The last twelve years of my life in England have been like everybody else's. I've been working hard making an honest living, raising you girls and obeying the rules. All my adventures feel like another lifetime, another me. Although, we went all around in England and Scotland, we saw countless castles and famous heritage sites, and we have been in Italy, France and Belgium with you girls, though of course those were family trips and not wild parties like in my youth.

When I went to Australia for three weeks to visit my best friend, Tigi, nothing unlawful happened to us and we hardly even got drunk despite all the partying and trouble we caused together on so many occasions when we were young.

Tigi & me enjoying the benefits of the hangover from last night

From his home in Sydney, we drove up to Pialba and stopped and spent nights at places like Coffs Harbour, Byron Bay and Gold Coast, where we spent most of our time.

We visited many conservation areas and national parks and they were beautiful, but, unfortunately, I didn't see any koalas. I was just a normal tourist. There were no fights, probably a few late nights but no arrests, either. Even so, I had a great time and I hope that I can visit Tigi at least one more time.

I've travelled with friends to many places in England and away from England. We went to Lisbon, Portugal, once, to see a football match – Portugal v Hungary – and of course to Hungary and some of those trips came very close to the parties I used to enjoy when I was young. I will spare you the details now.

I think the most interesting adventure was in Tenerife, in the Canary Islands. Eight of us went there to a stag party. Of course, I spent my first night in the police station but for a completely different reason than when I was young and what you kids think after reading my story this far. Let me tell you all about it.

We started drinking in the airport departure lounge, we continued drinking on the plane and didn't stop when we reached our rented luxury villa with swimming pool. The weather was hot so everybody was drinking around the pool. I had too much to drink and fell asleep on a sun bed. The next thing I remember is that I was gasping for air and fighting to reach the surface of the water. A friend of mine had thrown me in the pool with my sun bed while I was asleep. That wouldn't have been a problem but I had my mobile in my pocket and it wasn't waterproof. I always take screen shots of the places I stay so if I get lost – which happens all the time –I know where to go.

Anyway, we were drinking a lot and I think four of us decided to go into the town. I was in a bar playing pool and then the next thing I remember is walking along the street by myself, barefoot with my broken flip-flop in my hand. I thought, OK, let's go home. I felt my mobile in my pocket so I thought I would find the address and grab a taxi. The problem was that I couldn't open my mobile, either with my fingerprint or a code. What the fuck? I tried and tried but nothing happened. Shit! The only thing left to do was just wander the streets hoping that I would find my friends or the place where we were staying.

I was drunk, tired, my feet were hurting and it seemed like I had wandered for hours, unable to find anybody. The only thing I found after hours of walking was the police station. Then I realised that I could go in, ask them to call Anita – the only number I know by heart for emergencies – and she could find the address for me. Great idea! I went in and asked them to call Anita. They had WhatsApp, too, so I called her but there was no answer.

Everybody was very nice to me at the police station, even though I looked like a very drunk homeless guy. I probably stank too. They tried to call Anita every ten minutes but it was 3 o'clock in the morning so her phone was in silent mode and she was asleep. The police sat me down in the hallway, brought me a drink and a sandwich around 6:00am, and, of course, they kept calling Anita. I was bored out of my mind by the time my phone rang, probably around 7:00am.

Holy shit, it was a miracle! It was one of my friends asking where I was. As it happened, none of us had made it back to the villa. My friend told me where we were staying, so I said goodbye to the nice policemen and women and grabbed a taxi. I was almost at the address when I spotted my friends, so I joined them. They had been walking all night trying to find the villa but none of them had a phone with them, so they couldn't call anyone to find out where we were staying. Then I discovered that the phone I had actually belonged to my friend and that was why I couldn't open it. He was the luckiest because I kept his phone safe. The rest of the group lost their phones. So that's how I spent my first night in a police station without being charged for some kind of crime.

Feri and me when Albion beat Arsenal 2:1, happy times.

Feri came here twice from Canada – for an Albion vs. Arsenal football match and for a 'Tankcsapda' (Tank Trap) concert.

Besides my trips from England, some of my friends and even my brother came to see us. Tigi visited us once from Australia, Menyus, and even his daughter came from Hungary, Feri, came here twice from Canada – for an

And my brother came for his son Tommy's wedding. Now that was fun. He was supposed to get here a day early but by the time he reached the airport in Toronto, he was drunk. At the gate the 'gate keeper' told him that he stank. Instead of shutting his mouth, my brother told her, 'You stink too but you don't hear me complaining'.

From there the situation escalated to the point where my brother got arrested and put in a holding cell. He was lucky because they let him on a plane the next day, so he got here a few hours before the wedding. He started drinking heavily even though I asked him to slow down.

My brother & me before he got pissed as hell

He was OK at the wedding but at the party afterwards he looked very bad. We left the party early because of you girls but my brother stayed. The next morning, I had lots of messages on my phone from people I didn't know, saying that my brother was with them and that I should collect him because he was very drunk. So Anita and I went to the last place he had been seen in Brighton. As soon as we parked the car, the police called and told us where they were keeping him.

We went to pick him up and then the police told us that he was wandering in the middle of the road and when a driver asked him to get off the road because it was dangerous, my brother just hit him. The police let him go without arresting him but they asked us to take him home and put him in bed until he sobered up.

A few days later, we went to a pub with my friends to see a football match, and by the end of the game my brother was very drunk again. When we decided to go home, he wanted to eat some fried calamari. It wouldn't have been a problem if I had known where to get it. He was so drunk that he could have passed out at any moment, so I didn't want to wander around town looking for stupid calamari. I wasn't even driving because one of my friends had picked us up. I told my brother to eat something else, but he didn't want anything else.

Luckily, he got into the car but then he didn't stop picking on me because of the calamari. The fight continued at home and he got so angry that he packed up his stuff and left. We hadn't seen each other for years and he left because of fucking fried calamari! After a few nights in a hostel, he called me and we made peace. The rest of his visit was great. We went to town to look around, I took him to London and Lewes, Tommy invited us for a family BBQ, and he spent some quality time with you girls, too.

Just recently, I went to Scotland on a whisky tour with two friends and on the way back we stayed in Blackpool. Because Árpi lives in Preston, he was able to come over for a night. I hadn't seen him for years. We met at the place we were staying and after a few drinks we headed into town. It was walking distance, so we didn't have to drive. We talked a lot and went from pub to pub. As it was a Saturday night, the town was very busy. We even made some 'friends' in one of the pubs, and we listened to live music in another one, so the evening was great. But after the pub, the next thing I remember is wandering on the street by myself again. I told you, girls, it happens to me all the time. I've got lost in Scotland two nights before, too. Somehow we had become separated, but this time I had my phone and I found my way back to the place where we were staying. I was the last one to get back.

The most dangerous thing to happen that weekend took place the next morning as Árpi was going home. I walked him to his car and we said goodbye, but when he was backing out of the parking spot, he touched the car behind him. He got out and we inspected the car but there was no damage, so he got back into his car. At that moment, a high and very drunk couple came over to us and told us that they were calling the police. It wasn't even their car, but still we showed them that there was no damage on the car so there was nothing to do. Still, these idiots called the police and they stopped Árpi. I think Árpi took a picture of the car and showed it to the police -- or somehow the police found out that there was no damage on the other car and let Árpi go free.

I have always been grateful to the UK for granting me citizenship, and I have always felt very at home here and welcome, at least until Brexit threw the country into so much turmoil. I have experienced racism first-hand, however. Because I still have a noticeable Hungarian accent, people have told me to go back to where I came from. Which raises a big question. Where would that be? Hungary, Italy, Austria, Spain, Germany, Canada?

I suppose they mean Hungary, but I find such blind hatred totally baffling. When I spent all those years travelling around Europe and living in Canada, I did so with a happy innocence. I felt so lucky to be alive and to have escaped from the privations of a harsh Communist regime and my natural instinct was always to try to make friends with people rather than to mistrust them or look down on them.

They say travel broadens the mind, but I have always been a people person, trying to make connections with others rather than build barriers. So I find Brexit totally alien and very hard to handle. I can understand intellectually and politically what makes people turn against each other, driven by what they read in their red top tabloid newspapers and the divide-and-rule policy of our venal and corrupt politicians, but I firmly believe that when we meet each other one-to-one, all those fears and prejudices can be overcome with kindness and humour and a love of life.

Some of the best times of my life took place in the company of an eclectic bunch of refugees from many different countries. On the whole, if we were good people, we looked out for each other, because we had so little; but in many ways, we were more free than most because we existed in a sub-culture at the fringes of society, outside of the rat race, free to think for ourselves, free to make impulsive decisions, free to cross borders illegally and free to visit a friend a thousand miles away by just hopping on a train. Not being tied down, we looked at the uncertainty of whatever the next day would bring more as an adventure than something to worry about or ruin our day.

Yes, that's it. I definitely worry a lot more now. I suppose that comes with living like everyone else – being, as it were, part of the Social Contract. Of course I have huge regret that I haven't seen you dear Krisztina and Attila for nearly twenty years. It is head-and-shoulders the biggest regret of my life. I don't know what I could have done differently at the time. Fight through the courts for access rights to you kids who lived half way around the globe with a mother who daily poisoned your minds against your own father? Besides, I had a new family with Anita and it took all my energy to provide for them and to be a good husband and father.

Time just rolls on until now, here we are after two decades apart and I have two grown-up estranged children: you Krisztina are 29, and you Attila are 26. I can't help feeling that if you wanted to track me down you would have done so by now, but maybe there is still time. Living through your twenties is solipsistic – I should know – so maybe when you are older and have your own children, you might come looking for me. If you ever read this book – I want you to know that my door and my heart are always open to you, no matter how many years have separated us.

The end – or maybe another beginning…

01 Szeged, Hungary – Latina, Italy

29/09/1986 (Monday): During my leave after the military oath, I fled across the Röszke-Horgos border to Yugo-slavia. I called my brother from Subotica in Italy to come and get me. In the evening, I went to Belgrade by train and, as we agreed, I waited for him at the train station at 6pm on Wednesday evening and every second hour after that.

30/09/1986 (Tuesday): I arrived in Belgrade and was there until 10am Thursday morning when my brother got there with his Polish friend, Tomek. We headed back to Italy that evening.

03/10/1986 (Friday): We arrived in Sežana at dawn and fled to Italy on foot. We spent the first night in Venice, where a gay guy gave us accommodation because he liked Tomek.

04/10/1986 (Saturday): In the morning our "landlord" left earlier than we did so we had the opportunity to search his apartment for hashish. I had never seen hashish before so my brother had to explain what to look for and I found it. We took a little for ourselves and then left the apartment. We went sightseeing a little bit and headed to Bologna where we spent the night. We wanted to sleep in an abandoned house in the suburbs but it was already occupied. We were scared and ran away. Eventually we slept under a bridge.

05/10/1986 (Sunday): In the morning we set off for Perugia and slept there as well.

06/10/1986 (Monday): We arrived in Latina (one of the cities in Italy where refugees could stay and where my brother was staying) and I stayed there until Christmas.

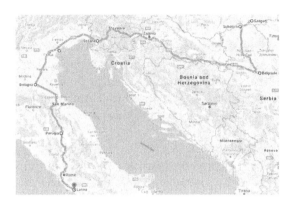

02 Latina, Italy – Göttschach, Austria

24/12/1986 (Wednesday): We set off to Austria from Latina for the holidays to surprise our friends but our first run was unsuccessful. We were caught on the train to the border and turned back.

25/12/1986 (Thursday): We were in Latina again.

26/12/1986 (Friday): We set off to Austria again but now with a car and with our friend, Reaper. One of our other friends took us to the Tarvisio-Villach border, where at night in knee-deep snow, we fled to Austria through the mountains.

27/12/1986 (Saturday): At dawn we were caught by the Austrian border guards/patrols when we were warming up at the train station. But because we told them that we escaped from Hungary through Yugoslavia and trying to reach Traiskirchen (all political refugees had to go there first to register), they let us go and even gave us free train tickets. We only travelled to Vienna because that is where our friends lived and because we didn't want to register to stay in Austria. We didn't even tell the border guards and patrols our real name. I was Zoltán Kovács (kovács means "blacksmith" in English and is a very common name in Hungary).

12/31/1986 (Wednesday): My first "trip" (LSD) party. It was very good.

03/01/1987 (Saturday): I changed my mind and registered in Traiskirchen and was in quarantine until 19/01/1987, and then I roamed with my friends in Austria.

25/02/1987 (Wednesday): We were drunk and loud in a small village where my friend, Gyula Gulyás (gulyás means "goulash" in English) was living and someone called the police on us. They locked me up in Linz because I was in the middle of changing my name back to the original so I didn't have an ID card. They just assumed that I was in Austria illegally. This wasn't true but the police didn't even bother to call the Traiskirchen camp to check my story.

24/04/1987 (Friday): I was released and went to Traiskirchen to look for friends. I slept a night there. I was given one week to leave Austria.

25/04/1987 (Saturday): My friend Güzü (güzü is a kind of field mouse) lived in Göttschach, so I went there and stayed with him.

03 Göttschach, Austria – Rome, Italy

05/05/1987 (Tuesday): My friend Deák (deák means "student" in English) drove me to the Villach-Tarvisio border where I fled to Italy at night.

06/05/1987 (Wednesday): I went to the police in Ferrara and told them that I had just escaped from Hungary through Yugoslavia and I wanted to go to Latina to register as a refugee. Of course, I had to use a different name again to get a free train ticket because I'd already registered as a refugee with my original name. At that time I was Zoltán Boldog (boldog means "happy" in English). A friend of mine told me to use that name because I was always smiling. I spent the night with my brother in a hotel in Latina where he was staying.

07/05/1987 (Thursday): I registered as a refugee in Latina again. I was there for about one month while I registered with Canada so I could go there to live.

01/06/1987 (Sunday): I moved to Rome and in the next four months I lived in two different hotels.

04 Rome, Italy – Barcelona, Spain

04/10/1987 (Sunday): I left for Spain with two friends, Csaszi and Leslie.

05/10/1987 (Monday): We arrived in Ventimiglia. We waited until dark and took a bus to the border. Unfortunately, the bus stop was about five metres from the border and every border guard/patrol saw us getting off and turning around and heading back where we came from. We still managed to cross the border to Menton, France but because we were spotted at the border earlier due to our clumsiness, several border guards/patrols were looking for us in Menton in civilian clothes and of course, they caught us. That night we slept in custody at the border.

06/10/1987 (Tuesday): We were thrown back to Italy in the morning. We went to Genoa and stayed there for two nights. Since we had run out of money, one of my friends, Leslie, decided to go back to Rome. This came in very handy for us as it allowed him to lock us up in the "tube". Hungarian refugees named the overhead area of the train (where all the wires, pipes and other things that ran services for the train) the "tube". In the toilet's ceiling there was an access panel that could be opened with pliers from below and with a hand from above and two people could fit up there. Refugees used the "tube" to cross borders without detection.

08/10/1987 (Thursday): Leslie locked us up in the "tube" at dawn and we arrived in Nice that morning. We continued our journey to Spain by hitchhiking. We broke into a small Italian coffee kiosk on the beach near Toulon and we spent our first night there. When we left in the morning we stole a lots of frozen pizza and we lived on it for a while because we had no money and we were hungry.

09/10/1987 (Friday): We got to Marseille and slept on the beach there too, but now outdoors. It was freezing cold.

10/10/1987 (Saturday): We slept near Montpellier at the end of a small village in a gas station's office.

11/10/1987 (Sunday): We neared Narbonne, where a Spanish gypsy brigade (caravans) stopped us and offered to give us food, accommodation and 50 francs a day if we helped them pick grapes. It's true that it wasn't the best deal, but we were hungry, tired and broke, so we took the deal.

12/10/1987 (Monday): We started work and worked there until 16/10/1987 (Friday).

17/10/1987 (Saturday): The gypsies took us to Narbonne from where we took a train to Cerbére. As soon as it got dark we crossed the border to Portbou, Spain and the next morning we took a train to Barcelona.

18/10/1987 (Sunday): We arrived in Barcelona by train. We were drinking, sightseeing and slept on the beach at night.

19/10/1987 (Monday): We registered as refugees with Barcelona Red Cross. We needed a translator and when he arrived, my friend almost stopped breathing. He was just poking me and saying "look, look who our translator is!" I had no idea, because I wasn't a big football fan. Our translator was one of the most famous Hungarian football players who ever lived, Zoltán Czibor who played for the Golden Team. I lived in 4 places in Barcelona.

03/03/1988 (Thursday): I received my benefit from the Spanish government through Red Cross and I went to Madrid because I found out that two of my best friends from Szeged, Hungary (Tigi, Szkuri) were there. I spent my evening on the bus.

04/03/1988 (Friday): I arrived in Madrid and I stayed there for about one month.

01/04/1988 (Friday): I went back to Barcelona for my monthly benefits. I spent a night in the train's "tube" because I didn't have any money for the ticket.

02/04/1988 (Saturday): I arrived in Barcelona and picked up my benefits.

03/04/1988 (Sunday): Zozi's parents came from Hungary and brought a package for me from my parents. In the evening Zozi's father quarrelled with me so I left our hotel.

04/04/1988 (Monday): I left for Madrid at 10:00am and arrived there by the evening. I stayed there for a month and a half and then moved back to Barcelona with my two friends (Tigi, Szkuri).

23/05/1988 (Monday): We left for Barcelona and slept on the bus.

24/05/1988 (Tuesday): We arrived in Barcelona. Until the beginning of August we lived in two places.

02/08/1988 (Tuesday): We were kicked out from the hotel, so we went down to the Costa Brava and slept rough on the beach. We usually slept in Calella and sometimes in Barcelona but always on the beach.

19/08/1988 (Friday): In Calella, Zozi and I stole two women's handbags because we had no money. The police later arrested me and my poor friend Szkuri, who had nothing to do with the robbery. We spent two nights in a prison in Calella and then we were transferred to a prison in Lloret de Mare, where we spent three days until we were found guilty. On day four we were transferred to a jail in Barcelona. Szkuri was taken to a juvenile prison because he wasn't 21 years old yet. We were in prison for 45 days.

07/10/1988 (Friday): We were released and found each other that night. We spent our night walking and talking. The next day we found our friends and partied with them. We spent our second "free" night on the street again because Zozi got into a fight with his girlfriend and the owner of the hotel threw us out as we had no money to pay for the night. I had a $150 (Canadian) cheque sent by my brother but because of the weekend I couldn't even collect my money so on our third "free" night we slept on the street again. Monday finally came and I got my money. We moved into a hotel and stayed there until we left Spain.

05 Barcelona, Spain – Vienna, Austria

26/11/1988 (Saturday): My friend Szkuri and I left for Germany but we planned to go to Rome and Vienna first to meet up with my friends. We left by train in the afternoon and were already in Portbou by evening. We crossed the border on foot at night to Cerbére.

27/11/1988 (Sunday): In the morning we took a train from Cerbére and continued on our way. In two days we reached Monaco and from there we walked all the way to Ventimiglia.

29/11/1988 (Tuesday): We arrived in Ventimiglia. We took a train to Sanremo. We dropped off our luggage in the luggage storage and went to Imperia to the police station and told them that somebody had stolen our luggage, which contained our passport and money. They gave us a free train ticket to Rome so we could go to the Hungarian Embassy where we could get help. That's exactly what we wanted because we didn't have any money but we wanted to go to Rome to visit my friends. We went back to Sanremo for our luggage and from there we took the train straight to Rome. We partied through the night and I woke up in someone's car the next morning. We left for Vienna that afternoon. My friends locked us in the train's "tube". We traveled all night.

01/12/1988 (Thursday): We arrived in Vienna in the morning. We found our friends and settled down. We spent our time mostly in Vienna but visited friends in other cities and towns all over Austria.

18/01/1989 (Wednesday): I went to visit my friend Árpi in a small village near Amstetten and I stayed there overnight.

19/01/1989 (Thursday): We went over to a mutual friend in Amstetten and slept there.

20/01/1989 (Friday): We got very drunk and drew swastikas on cars and yelled "Sieg Heil" so someone called the police. Because I was in Austria illegally, I was arrested.

21/01/1989 (Saturday): I was transferred to the St. Pölten prison where I immediately went on hunger strike because they wanted to transfer me back to Hungary where ten years imprisonment was waiting for me because I had escaped from the military. I knew from other Hungarians that if I went on hunger strike they would release me after ten days because they didn't want to spend money on my healthcare and that ten days time is not enough to take care of the paperwork for my transfer to Hungary.

01/02/1989 (Wednesday): I was released because of the hunger strike. I went back to Vienna.

14/02/1989 (Tuesday): I was caught again by the police for staying in the country illegally. I spent the night in a lockup in Vienna.

15/02/1989 (Wednesday): I was transferred to the prison in Vienna where I learned that my friend Szkuri, who had been caught for stealing earlier, had been transferred back to Hungary. I also learned that if I swallowed something metal they would release me because they didn't want to spend money on my healthcare. I immediately swallowed the zipper of my bomber jacket so they would release me but unfortunately it didn't happen, so I went on hunger strike again.

25/02/1989 (Saturday): I was released and spent the night with my friends in Vienna.

06 Vienna, Austria – Tübingen, Germany

26/02/1989 (Sunday): I left for Germany with Tigi and Imi. We slept on the train.

27/02/1989 (Monday): We arrived in Bregenz. We waited until it got dark and headed for the border. We arrived in Lindau on the same night but there was no train, so we hid somewhere and waited for the morning.

28/02/1989 (Tuesday): We took the morning train to Überlingen where my friend Tigi lived. We stayed there all week until Sunday morning.

05/03/1989 (Sunday): We went to Freiburg to register as political refugees. We slept there one night. Imi didn't want to register so I continued my journey alone.

06/03/1989 (Monday): I went to the refugee camp in Karlsruhe and I lived there while my paperwork was done.

09/03/1989 (Thursday): I had been transferred to the Heilbron refugee camp. I was relocated to Stuttgart sometime in July but I never slept there.

I roamed the country a lot but outside the camp I only spent a long time in Überlingen and Tübingen. With the help of a couple of acquaintances, I cheated the Volks Bank out of 7,500 marks. Since it was all their idea and not mine, we agreed that I would use my name for the whole thing and in return they would get me a German passport and an aeroplane ticket to Toronto. Unfortunately, they ripped me off and gave me nothing so I had to call my friend Péter for help. He had the size and temperament to threaten these bastards. They finally got me a passport and paid for all the expenses except the aeroplane ticket, for which my brother paid.

While I waited for my aeroplane ticket, I hid in a small hotel because I didn't want to get caught for the fraud I had committed. I was meant to keep a low profile but one night I decided to get drunk. I met a group of guys and we were drinking together and I bought some rounds too. Then, to avoid paying my bill, I climbed out of the toilet window and went back to my hotel to sleep. Luckily, I had told everyone in the pub where I lived, so the next morning the police woke me up. For some reason, I wasn't wanted yet for the fraud, so the police only took the money I owed at the pub and didn't arrest me. Since I was very lucky, I called my friend Péter and moved to Tübingen.

06/09/1989 (Wednesday): My last day in Tübingen. I spent the night with my friend Péter, who took me to France the next day.

07 Tübingen, Germany – Toronto, Canada

07/09/1989 (Thursday): We crossed the border to Strasbourg, France. Péter's passport and my fake one, in which I was called B. Volker, were placed on the dashboard so the border guards/patrols could see them through the windshield of the car and luckily, we were not stopped for further inspection. I took the evening train to Paris. I slept on the train.

08/09/1989 (Friday): I arrived in Paris in the morning. I found a hotel and went sightseeing around the city.

09/09/1989 (Saturday): I flew from Paris to Toronto to my brother. Due to the weather, we almost didn't go to Toronto, which would have been bad because my brother had his birthday that day. Luckily, after a long delay, we arrived in Toronto. To celebrate my arrival and my brother's birthday, he organised a party. He invited our friend Reaper from Montreal (we knew him from Italy), who invited another friend from Toronto, Miki.

The party went well until our friend Reaper came up with the idea of stealing a car so he could drive back to Montreal. I begged him not to do it as I had just arrived and didn't want any trouble, but no one listened to me.

We didn't manage to steal a car, but someone saw us behaving suspiciously and called the cops. We were arrested and since I had a German passport, I was not even released from the police lockup. The cops were jerks anyway, as Reaper tried to crack the car with a screwdriver, which he then threw away but the cops claimed our burglary tool was a metal clothes hanger which they found in the lock of the car.

ABOUT THE AUTHORS

ZOLTÁN MIHÁLY was born in Hungary in 1967. When he was 19 years old, he escaped from the Hungarian military and fled to Italy. In his absence, he was sentenced to 10 years in prison. In the next five years he was in many countries in Europe and USA until he settled down in Canada. He travelled with fake passports or without them at all. He now lives in England.

STEVE EGGLESTON is a law school Valedictorian, former law professor, author, lecturer, and colourful trial lawyer. In his renaissance life, he has launched a hip-hop start-up, produced feature films, helmed a rock 'n roll magazine, booked 1000+ live shows worldwide, and managed Grammy-winning artists. As an international bestselling author, he is published in fiction and non-fiction and lives with his family in Somerset, England, where he draws and paints in his free time. Steve's business can be found on steveegglestonwrites.com.

MIKE POWELL is a former RADA-trained professional actor, musical director and managing editor in book publishing. For the last 20 years he has been a best-selling author, with more than 135 non-fiction titles published by a wide range of industry leaders on topics as varied as world history, virulent diseases, international etiquette, serial killers, puzzles and brain training to popular culture, humour and the performing arts. He lives in Cardiff with his wife, their two grown-up children and a golden retriever called Douglas.

OTHER BOOKS FROM HUMMINGBIRD
PUBLISHING AUTHORS

Steve Eggleston
Conquering Your Adversaries
Writing Your Book After Covid-19
Destination 9/11
Conflicted
A Long Way Home

Michael Powell
The Little Book of Dumb Questions
Games on Thrones
Forbidden Knowledge
Mind Games
Acting Techniques: An Introduction for Aspiring Actors

Alison Rattle
Amelia Dyer: Angel Maker
V for Violet
The Quietness
The Madness
The Beloved

AVAILABLE TO BUY NOW FROM
HUMMINGBIRD BOOKS

A TRIP SPLATTER NOVEL

CONFLICTED

"Killer book. I loved every page of it.
CONFLICTED is a total winner on
every level. Great courtroom stuff,
great characters, great plot, narrative
mega-drive and - in Dave Splatter, P.I.
- a stand-alone hero for the ages."

–JOHN LESCROART
New York Times Bestselling author

矛
盾
的

Bestselling Author
STEVE EGGLESTON
WITH JOHN NEYER

AVAILABLE TO BUY NOW FROM
HUMMINGBIRD BOOKS

MAYUR KOTECHA
WITH ALISON RATTLE

30 DAYS
IN HEAVEN

Printed in Great Britain
by Amazon

79250187R00161